PRESCHOOL BIBLE CRAFTS

by
Kathy Darling

illustrated by Veronica Terrill

Shining Star Publications, Copyright © 1992

ISBN No. 0-86653-699-X

Standardized Subject Code TA ac

Printing No. 9876543

Shining Star Publications
A Division of Frank Schaffer Publications, Inc.
23740 Hawthorne Boulevard
Torrance, CA 90505-5927

The purchase of this book entitles the buyer to reproduce student activity pages for classroom use only. Any other use requires written permission from Shining Star Publications.

All rights reserved. Printed in the United States of America.

Unless otherwise indicated, the New International Version of the Bible was used in preparing the activities in this book.

DEDICATION

To my dear friend Janice, for her patience, love, and support.

TABLE OF CONTENTS

In the Beginning 7
Little Lights 8
Creation, a Banner Week 9
Adam and Eve Pop-Up 17
Temptation's Hand/That Slinky Snake 20
The Angel at the Gates 23
Noah's Floating Zoo 25
A Colorful Covenant! 30
Rainbows 'Round the Wrist 32
Rebekah's Water Jug 33
Jacob's Ladder 34
Coat of Many Colors 36
Seven Years of Famine 38
The Chain of Israel 41
Moses, Moses Gently down the Nile 42
The Burning Bush 44
The Sea Divides 45
The Trumpet Sounds! 46
The Ten Commandments 47
From the Heart, a Commandment Collage 50
The Land of Milk and Honey 51
A Feast of Milk and Honey 53

The Sun Stood Still	54
Chariots of Iron	56
Samson	58
Gideon, the Miracle of the Messenger	60
The Dew on the Fleece	62
David and Goliath	64
Jonah's Whale of a Time	66
Gabriel Visits Mary	69
Tools of the Trade	70
The Ride to Bethlehem	72
The Christ Child	74
Three Wise Men	75
The Mustard Seed	79
Little Fish in the Sea	80
Little Lost Lamb	82
Feeding Five Thousand	84
Jesus Rides into Jerusalem	85
The Last Supper	87
Oh, Peter!	89
Crown of Thorns	90
Jesus on the Cross	92
Jesus Is Risen!	93
Resources, Picture Books	94
Resources, Hands-On Crafts and Activities	95
Resources, Familiar Tunes, Music	96

INTRODUCTION

With *Preschool Bible Crafts* you can bridge the gap between the real and unreal. Bible stories and concepts are often difficult for very young children to comprehend. Learning by doing gives them an altogether different view of the many Bible heroes, puzzling parables, and loving lessons of our Lord. The richness of the Bible will come to life as they create with their own hands a key ingredient or visual reminder of the material you introduce. These handmade products—crafts, colorings, and constructions—will provide an outlet for creative energies as well as a source of self-esteem and pride in a job well-done.

Almost all the materials needed for the products in this book are inexpensive and found easily and quickly in most variety stores. Craft stores are great places for inspiration and excellent sources for materials, but most items required for our purposes need not be purchased from a specialty store. You will note that many materials can be collected from around the home. If your children love arts and crafts as much as mine, it is a good idea to get in the habit of collecting all empty milk and egg cartons, strawberry baskets, cardboard tubes, various fabric and ribbon scraps, and anything else that might be used as the basis for a new creation. You might send a note home to parents asking them to start collecting as well.

Common kitchen items such as coffee filters, straws, toothpicks, paper napkins, paper lunch bags, pasta products, and even dry cereals can all be used sooner or later. Don't overlook anything! I would suggest making one significant investment—the purchase of a large container of good, strong craft glue. Tacky Glue is wonderful, hangs tough, and can be thinned with a little water when it gets too thick. If an oven is handy, it is always a help to place finished crafts on a cookie sheet in an oven set on a very low temperature until they are dry. This way the children may take home their works of art without their being in danger of self-destructing before they get there. Just remember to watch the oven!

Each craft project begins with directions, with the materials listed in the Gather Up section. Get Ready lets you know about any preparation needed before the children begin. Go is where the children take over. Be sure to read through the entire activity before beginning. With any learning adventure for preschoolers, you will need to be involved through the whole process. However, take a backseat when you can, and cheer them on when you do! At this age, skill levels vary greatly. Some children are good with cutting; some have not mastered scissor skills at all. Assess the needs and abilities of your group before beginning. As always, take into consideration the maturity of your group before deciding which activities will be both safe and rewarding. *(I am always concerned with letting very little ones work with scissors or very small objects that might find their way to their mouths. Please keep this in mind.)*

Patterns are provided at the end of each craft, accompanied by Bible verses to use as Bible story references. As you consult these references, you will see that some sections of the Bible text are suitable for reading to the children. Others, because of vocabulary or wording, may be inappropriate. There are many excellent Bible story collections that speak directly to children in a language they can understand. These and other picture books, as well as ideas for crafts and music, are included in the Resource section (page 95). Try to expand your lesson, using as many resources as you can. When a well-rounded lesson reaches the children through hands-on crafts, literature, music, and other disciplines, the impact can be immeasurable!

As a Christian preschool teacher or parent, you play an important role in the lives of the young children you teach. Thank you for being where you are, and for taking the time to share your life and energy with the children of our world. You are feeding the hearts and souls of our future. So get out the paint, craft sticks, glue, and glitter, and have fun!

"And God said, 'Let there be light,' and there was light."   Genesis 1:3

IN THE BEGINNING

Gather Up: 1 1/2" to 2" Styrofoam balls, silver and gold glitter, silver and gold metallic pipe cleaners, craft glue, scissors, two small shallow dishes

Get Ready: Cut the pipe cleaners into 2" sections. Pour silver and gold glitter into a dish and mix. Pour glue into another small dish.

Go: Have children roll balls around in the glue to coat them. Then they drop the balls in the glitter dish and roll them around again to coat them. They gently pick up the balls and poke the pipe cleaner sections into them. They may set their sparkly decorations in the window as glittery reminders of the Lord's gift of light.

Note: It's a good idea to provide a couple of plain balls and some pipe cleaner sections so children can practice poking them in. Show them how to hold the pipe cleaner close to the bottom, then push it in firmly with one stroke.

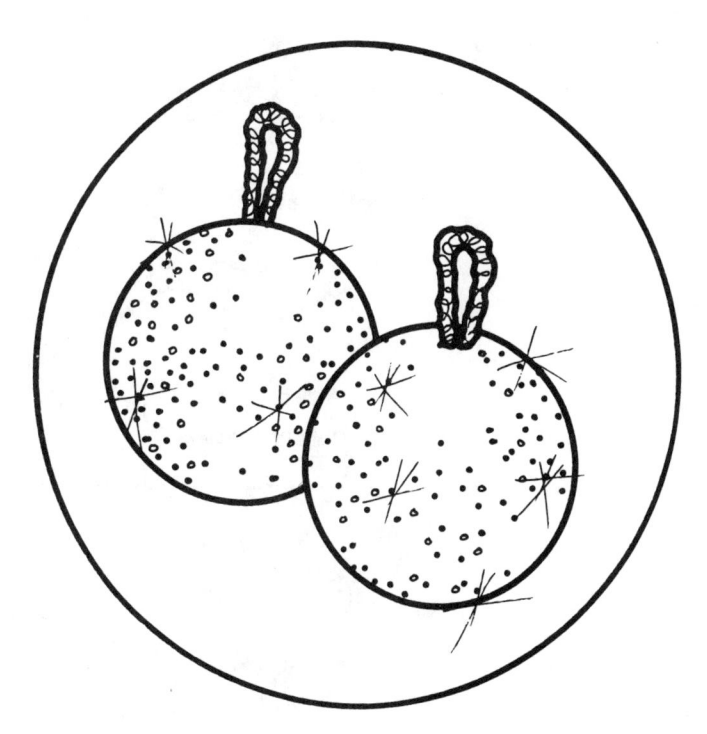

"God saw that the light was good . . . ." Genesis 1:4

LITTLE LIGHTS

Gather Up: Petroleum jelly, gold glitter, teaspoon, bowl, cotton-tipped swabs, paper towels

Get Ready: Put a few spoonfuls of petroleum jelly in a bowl, pour in some glitter, and mix.

Go: Let children celebrate the first light of the universe by painting each other's faces! They may dip swabs into the glitter mixture and carefully spread it across cheeks or on noses. Make sure they are careful to keep swabs away from eyes. The sparkles will wipe off easily with tissues or paper towels. Let children wear their sparkles as reminders to pass on the Lord's love light!

Note: Assess your group's maturity and self-control before deciding to let them handle the swabs. Some groups might be better with adults doing the painting.

CREATION, A BANNER WEEK

Gather Up: Patterns, seven white paper plates, crayons, adhesive stars, glitter, glue, scissors, stapler

Get Ready: Make copies of the patterns for all your students.

Go: Follow the directions at the bottom of each pattern page and help children color and/or decorate them. Younger children may need help cutting out the circles. Let them glue finished circles to the centers of paper plates. Staple the plates end to end, with the first day starting on the left. Encourage children to tack up their banners at home.

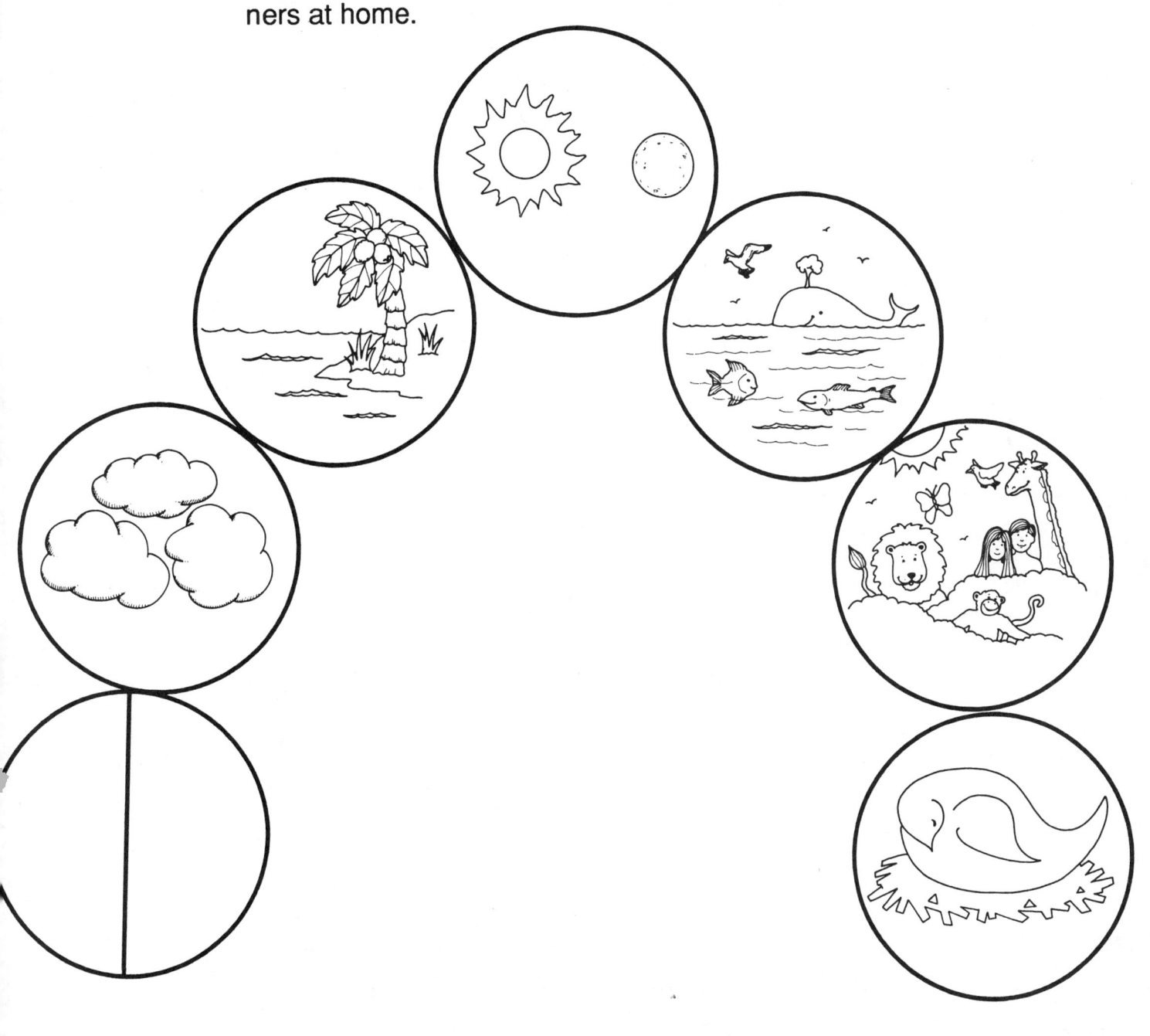

"God called the light 'day,' and the darkness he called 'night.' And there was evening, and there was morning—the first day." Genesis 1:5

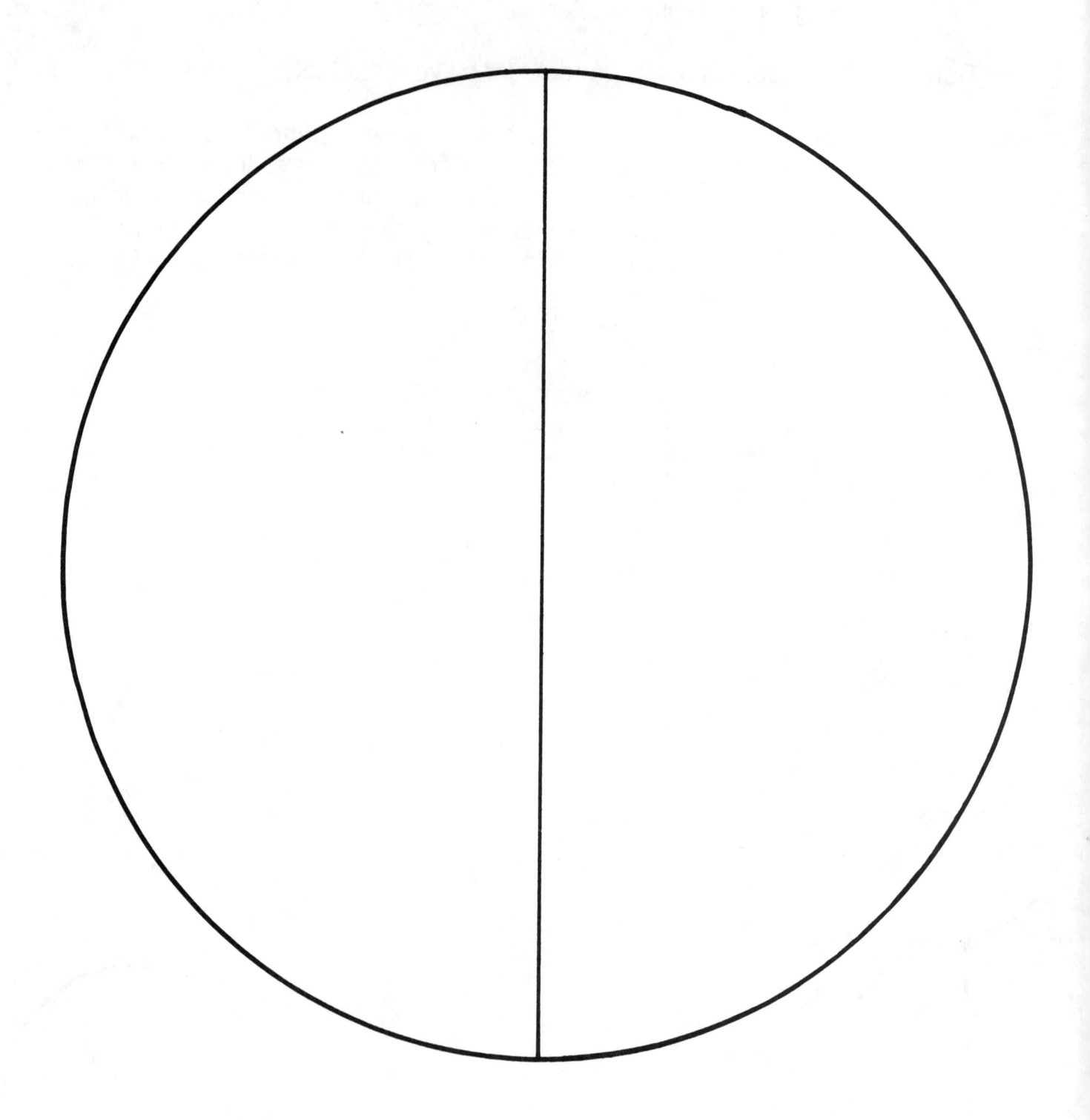

Color one side of the circle black; leave the other side blank.

"God called the expanse 'sky.' And there was evening, and there was morning—the second day." Genesis 1:8

Color the circle blue.

"God called the dry ground 'land,' and the gathered waters he called 'seas.' And God saw that it was good." Genesis 1:10

"The land produced vegetation: . . . and trees bearing fruit . . . . And there was evening, and there was morning—the third day." Genesis 1:12-13

Color the picture.

"God made two great lights—the greater light to govern the day and the lesser light to govern the night. He also made the stars." Genesis 1:16

"And there was evening, and there was morning—the fourth day." Genesis 1:19

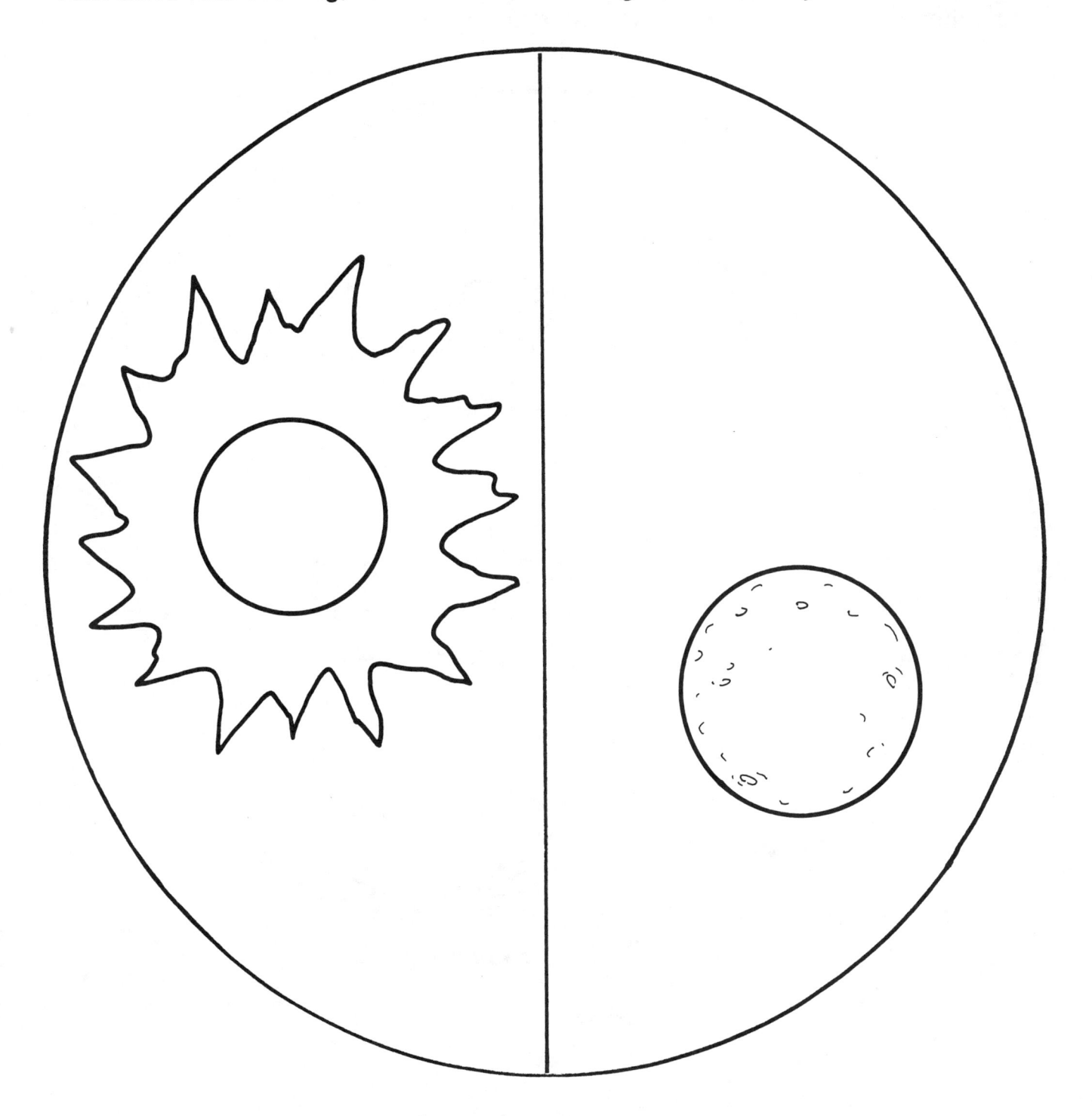

Color the moon yellow; then press on some stars. If desired, color a black background around the moon and stars. Color the sun orange and yellow. If desired, color a blue background around the sun.

"So God created the great creatures of the sea and every living and moving thing with which the water teems, . . . and every winged bird . . . . And God saw that it was good." Genesis 1:21

"And there was evening, and there was morning–the fifth day." Genesis 1:23

Color the picture.

"God made the wild animals . . . the livestock . . . and all the creatures that move along the ground . . . ."   Genesis 1:25

"So God created man in his own image, in the image of God he created him; male and female he created them."   Genesis 1:27

"God saw all that he had made, and it was very good. And there was evening, and there was morning—the sixth day."   Genesis 1:31

Color the picture.

"... so on the seventh day he rested from all his work. And God blessed the seventh day and made it holy, because on it he rested from all the work...."

Genesis 2:2-3

Color the dove.

ADAM AND EVE POP-UP

Gather Up: The heart and figure patterns, 9" x 12" red or pink construction paper, yellow construction paper, scissors, tape, glitter, ribbon, stickers, crayons, glue

Get Ready: Fold the piece of yellow construction paper in half. Place the figure pattern on the fold and draw around it. Cut it out; then unfold to see two people holding hands. Cut one for each child. (Fold each outer arm backwards at the dotted lines.)

Fold the red or pink construction paper in half. Place the half-heart pattern on the fold. Trace it on the paper. Cut out and unfold the heart. Some children may be able to cut out the hearts for themselves.

On the inside, at the center of the heart, draw two dots about 3" apart.

Go: Have each child fold the heart closed and decorate the outside with glitter, stickers, or crayons. When it is dry, the child should open the heart and tape one arm of the "holding hands" figures to each dot. (The fold of the figures should be pointing out so that they "pop up" when the heart is opened.)

Note: This takes a bit of preparation, but it is well worth the effort. Children love to see the Adam and Eve figures pop up when they open their cards.

"So the man gave names to all the livestock, the birds of the air and all the beasts of the field. But for Adam no suitable helper was found."   Genesis 2:20

"So the Lord God caused the man to fall into a deep sleep; and while he was sleeping, he took one of the man's ribs . . . . Then the Lord God made a woman . . . and he brought her to the man. The man said, 'This is now bone of my bones and flesh of my flesh . . . .'"

Genesis 2:21-23

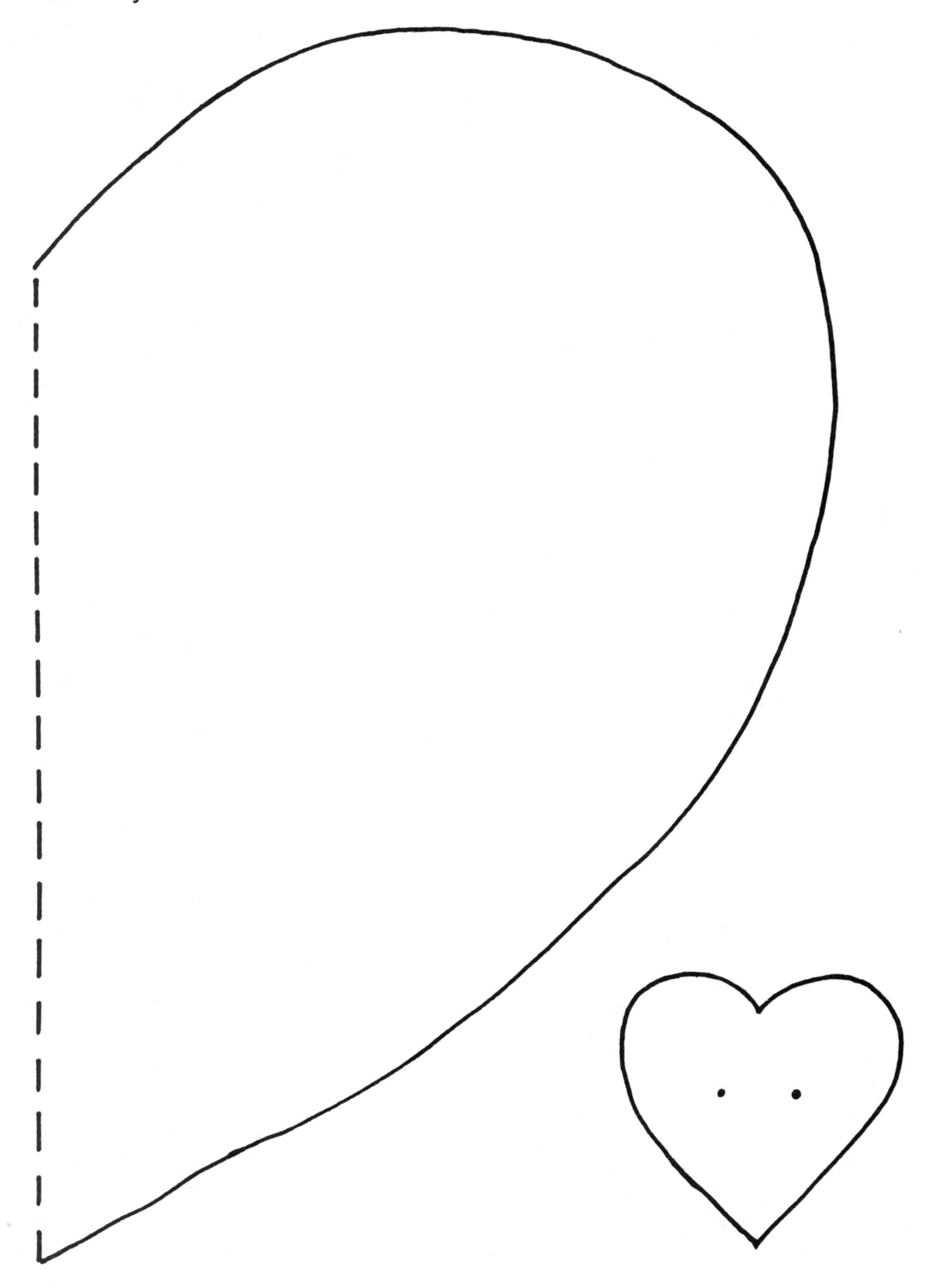

TEMPTATION'S HAND

Gather Up: Small snake and apple patterns, 9" x 12" white construction paper, crayons, scissors, glue, hole punch, yarn

Get Ready: Make a copy of the patterns for each student.

Go: Have children color the patterns and cut them out. Then have each trace a hand on white paper. Some may need assistance. Help each glue the snake to the hand near the wrist, and the apple over the fingers. Punch holes in the page and string with yarn to hang.

THAT SLINKY SNAKE

Gather Up: Coiled snake pattern, scissors, crayons, sequins, glue, hole punch, paper reinforcers, red yarn

Get Ready: Make a copy of the coiled snake pattern for each student and cut it out.

Go: Have the children color the snake. Starting at the tail, have each cut along the dotted line to make a snake spiral. Then the child may want to lay the snake down flat in its coiled shape and glue on a sequin eye or add several sequins to the body. Let the glue dry completely. Punch a hole at the mouth. Stick paper reinforcers on the front and back to secure the hole from tearing, and tie on a length of red yarn for hanging.

"... The woman said, 'The serpent deceived me, and I ate.'" Genesis 3:13

"So the Lord God said to the serpent, 'Because you have done this, Cursed are you . . . . You will crawl on your belly and you will eat dust all the days of your life.'"

Genesis 3:14

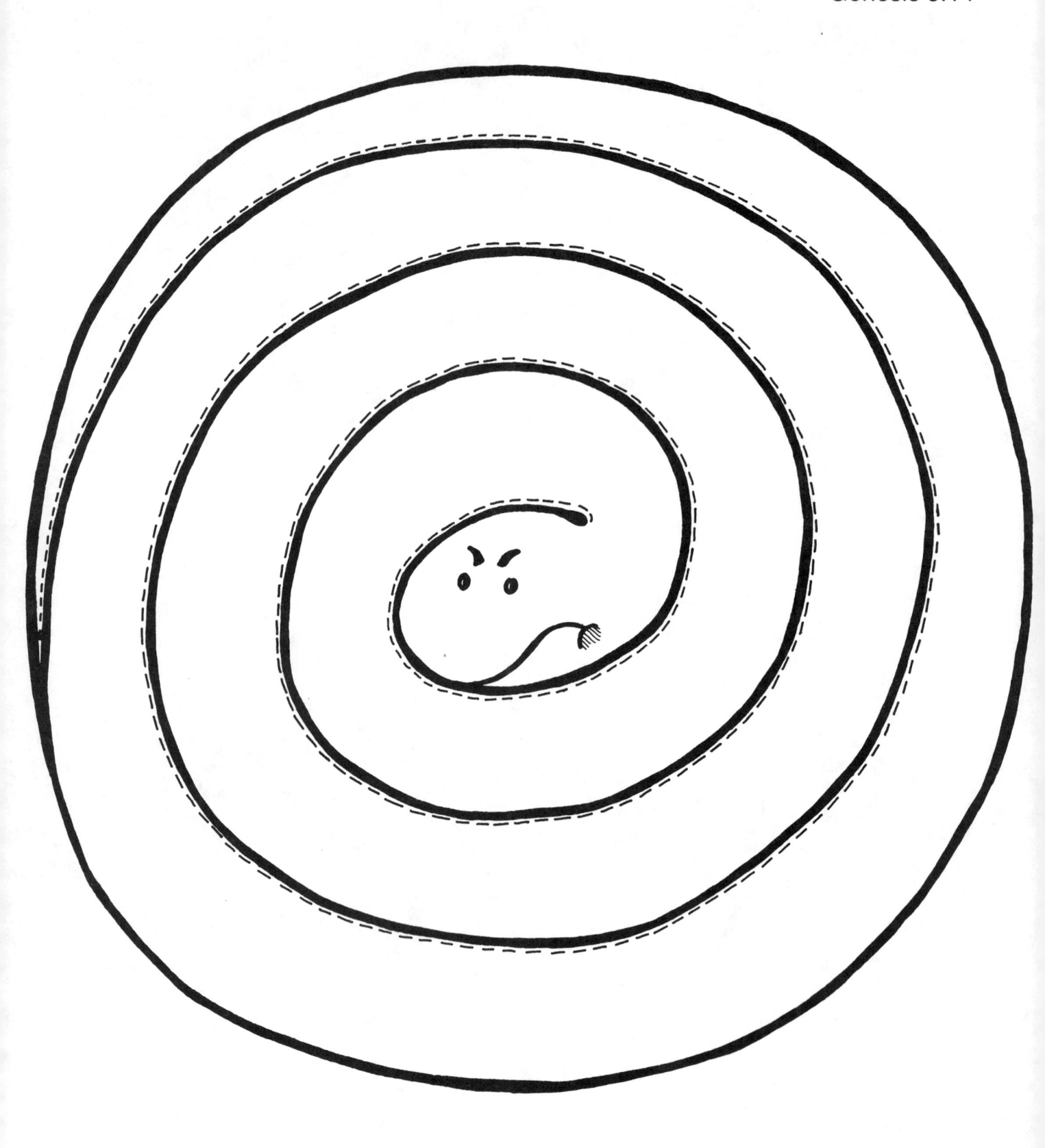

THE ANGEL AT THE GATES

Gather Up: Angel pattern, toilet tissue tubes, crayons, frilled party toothpick, pencil, scissors

Get Ready: Copy the angel pattern for each child. If necessary, cut it out.

Go: Have each child color an angel. Using a sharp pencil, poke small holes at the dots in the angel's hand. Help the child carefully insert the point of the toothpick in one hole and out the other. This is the angel's sword. The child may spread glue on the bottom half of the angel's back, and press it onto the tube to make it stand up.

"After he drove the man out, he placed on the east side of the Garden of Eden cherubim and a flaming sword flashing back and forth to guard the way to the tree of life."

Genesis 3:24

NOAH'S FLOATING ZOO

Gather Up: Ark and animal patterns, half-gallon milk cartons, toilet tissue tubes, 9" x 12" sheets of brown construction paper, crayons, scissors, glue

Get Ready: Make a copy of the window sections and the animals for each child. If necessary, cut them out for the children.

Fold a sheet of brown paper in half, place the ark roof pattern on the fold and cut out.

Cut the tube into four sections (like napkin rings).

Go: To make the ark, cut the top off the milk carton. (This will leave one end open for storing animals in the ark.) Then have each child coat one side of a sheet of brown paper with glue and press it over three sides of the carton. The uncovered side of the carton will serve as the bottom.

Next, let the child color the window sections and glue them to the sides of the ark. Make sure to keep the top edge of the window sections above the edge of the ark. Glue the ark roof to the top edges of the window sections. Let dry completely.

To make the ark animals, let the child color the animal patterns and cut them out. Each pattern should be glued around a tube to make a stand-up animal. Encourage children to use their arks and animals in imaginative play!

"... you will enter the ark—you and your sons and your wife and your sons' wives with you. You are to bring into the ark two of all living creatures ...."

Genesis 6:18-19

Fold back slightly and glue roof here.

Fold back slightly and glue roof here.

"... on that day all the springs of the great deep burst forth, and the floodgates of the heavens were opened. And rain fell on the earth forty days and forty nights."

Genesis 7:11-12

"... the water had dried up from the earth. Noah then removed the covering from the ark and saw that the surface of the ground was dry."   Genesis 8:13

"Bring out every kind of living creature that is with you—the birds, the animals, and all the creatures that move along the ground—so they can multiply on the earth and be fruitful and increase in number upon it."   Genesis 8:17

A COLORFUL COVENANT!

Gather Up: Pattern, puffy craft pom-poms, 6" lengths of ribbon or yarn the colors of the rainbow, construction paper, crayons, glue, scissors, hole punch, extra yarn or ribbon

Get Ready: Copy the pattern for each child. Cut a piece of construction paper a bit larger than the pattern for each child.

Go: Have children color each section of the pattern one color of the rainbow. You may show an example for them to copy, or allow them to arrange colors in their own unique spectrums. After coloring, have them cut out their strips or do this for them. Show them how to glue the ribbon ends to the bottom edge of the construction paper, and glue the rainbow-colored strips onto their papers. Then let children glue matching colored pom-poms to the colored sections. Punch a hole at the top of each child's creation and string with yarn to hang.

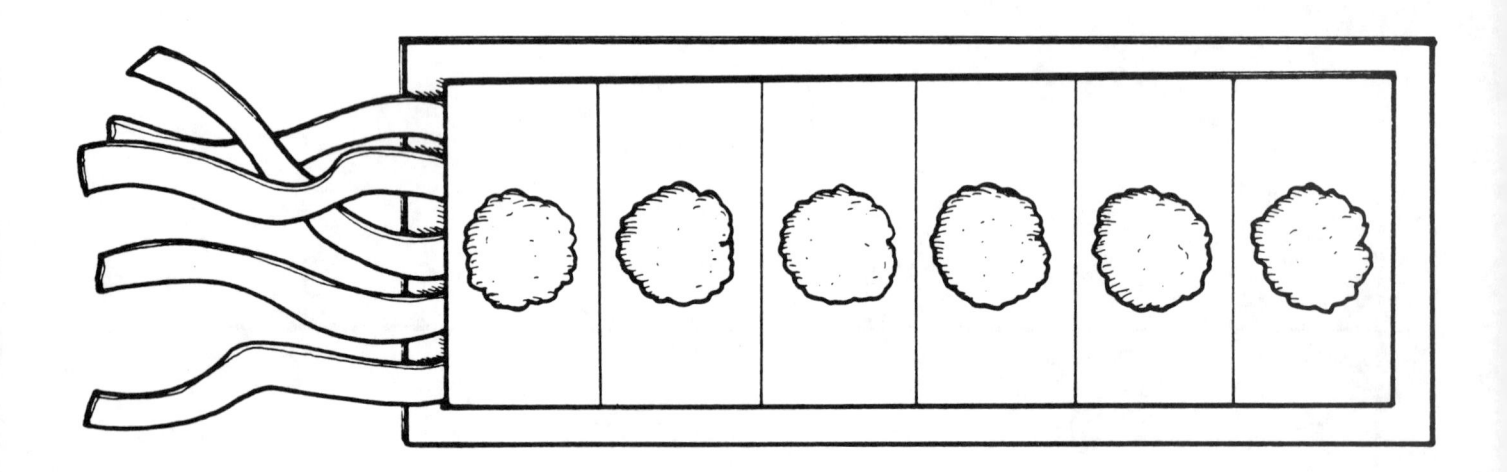

"I have set my rainbow in the clouds, and it will be the sign of the covenant between me and the earth." Genesis 9:13

purple
(violet)

blue

green

yellow

orange

red

"Whenever I bring clouds over the earth and the rainbow appears in the clouds"

Genesis 9:14

RAINBOWS 'ROUND THE WRIST

Get Ready: Glittery metallic pipe cleaners of varying colors, extra large sequins with holes (about the size of a nickel)

Get Set: Let each child choose a colored pipe cleaner for a bracelet.

Go: Have each child push six or seven colored sequins along the length of the pipe cleaner. Then help them fasten the pipe cleaners around their wrists by twisting and tucking under the ends. Tell children to wear their bracelets to remind them of the colorful covenant of promise that God placed in the sky after the flood.

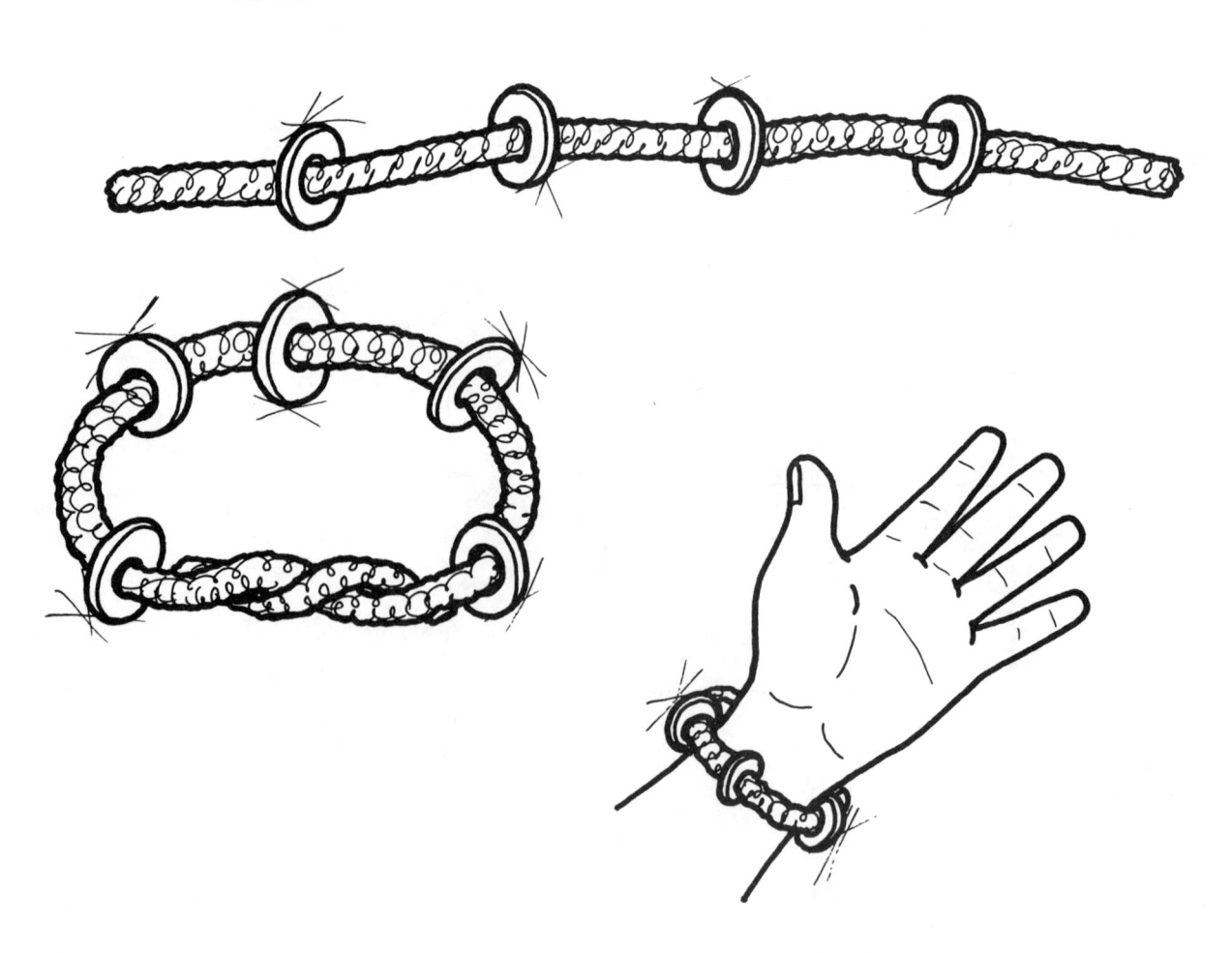

"May it be that when I say to a girl, 'Please let down your jar that I may have a drink,' and she says, 'Drink, and I'll water your camels too—'"   Genesis 24:14

REBEKAH'S WATER JUG

Gather Up: Plastic quart containers (cleaned and with labels removed), several colors of tissue paper, glossy craft glue, brushes, scissors

Get Ready: Cut colored tissue paper into random shapes. Put out bowls of glossy glue and brushes.

Go: Have children brush glue onto the containers. Then they may cover them with tissue paper pieces and smooth down the edges into the glue. They needn't worry about wrinkling. Some children may choose to make random bursts of color rather than cover the containers completely. Help them give the tissue a top coat of glossy glue. Let it dry completely. Encourage children to take their water jugs home, and perhaps use them to serve water to their families as reminders to be faithful servants of the Lord.

Note: One-quart juice containers work well.

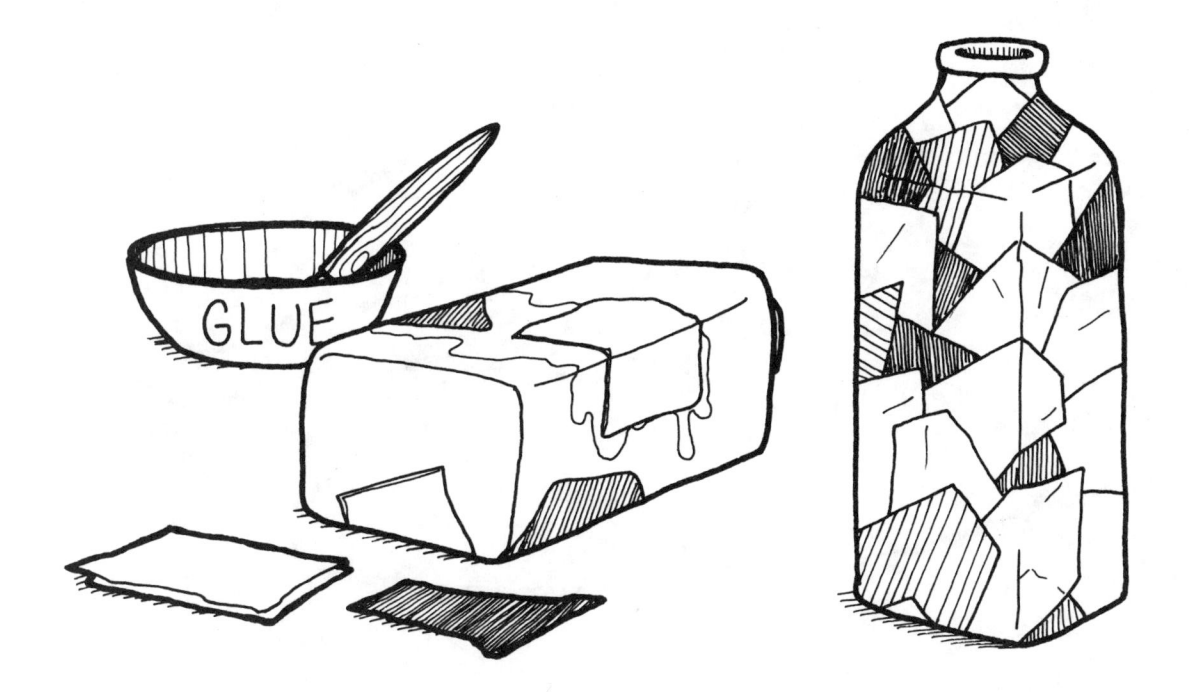

JACOB'S LADDER

Gather Up: Pattern, craft sticks, blue construction paper, crayons, scissors, glue, hole punch, yarn

Get Ready: Give each child two whole craft sticks and three halves. Using the pattern as a guide, cut cloud shapes from the blue paper a little larger than the pattern.

Go: Help each child place his two craft sticks parallel to one another. Put three dabs of glue on each stick at the top, the middle, and the bottom. Lay the half-sticks across to form a ladder. Let them dry. Meanwhile have the child color the pattern piece and cut it out. You may want to do this for some. The child glues the colored pattern on a blue cloud. When it is dry, he glues the cloud to the top of the ladder. String with yarn to hang.

"He had a dream in which he saw a stairway resting on the earth, with its top reaching to heaven, and the angels of God were ascending and descending on it." Genesis 28:12

"Then Jacob made a vow, saying, 'If God will be with me . . . so that I return safely to my father's house, then the Lord will be my God'" Genesis 28:20-21

COAT OF MANY COLORS

Gather Up: Pattern, ribbons or fabric strips, adhesive stars, black construction paper, crayons, scissors, glue, hole punch, yarn

Get Ready: If necessary, cut out a pattern for each child. Cut ribbons and narrow fabric strips into short lengths.

Go: Let children decorate Joseph's coat by filling in the stripes with ribbons and fabric or simply coloring it. They may fill in the stars with stickers. When dry, the colorful coat may be glued on black paper. String with yarn to hang.

"So when Joseph came to his brothers, they stripped him of his robe—the richly ornamented robe he was wearing—and they took him and threw him into the cistern...."   Genesis 37:23-24

"So when the Midianite merchants came by, his brothers ... sold him for twenty shekels of silver to the Ishmaelites, who took him to Egypt."   Genesis 37:28

"Then Jacob ... mourned for his son many days."   Genesis 37:34

SEVEN YEARS OF FAMINE

Gather Up: Patterns, popcorn kernels, 9" x 12" colored construction paper, crayons, scissors, glue, tacks

Get Ready: If necessary, cut out a number seven (after the children have colored it) and an ear of corn for each child.

Go: Have each child color the number seven, cut it out, and glue it to one side of a sheet of construction paper. Then each may color the withered ear of corn, cut it out, and glue it next to the seven. Show children how to glue seven kernels of popcorn to their withered ears of corn to represent the seven years of famine in Egypt.

"In my dreams I also saw seven heads of grain, full and good, growing on a single stalk. After them, seven other heads sprouted—withered and thin and scorched by the east wind. The thin heads of grain swallowed up the seven good heads . . . ."

Genesis 41:22-24

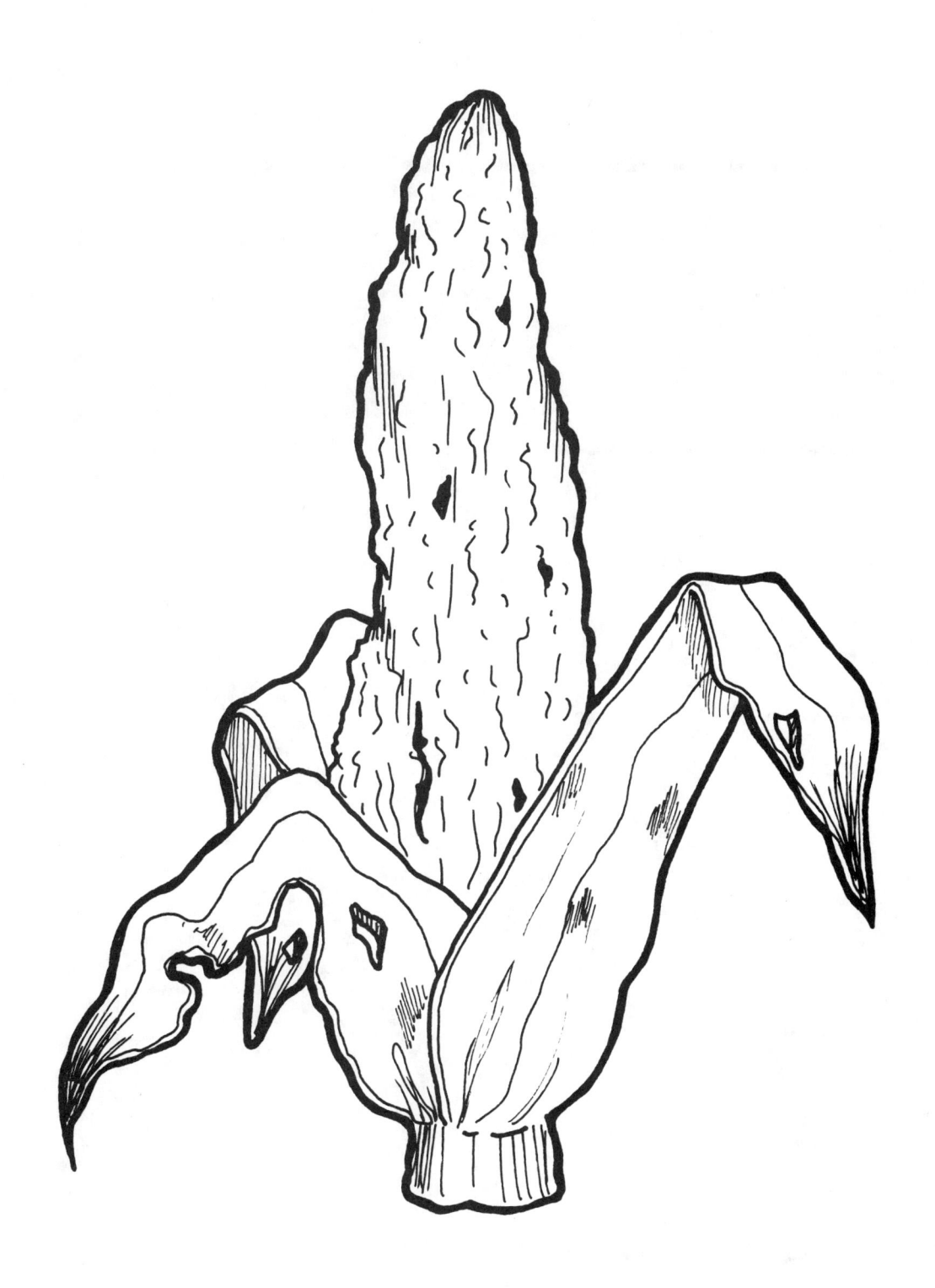

"Then Joseph said to Pharaoh, 'The dreams of Pharaoh are one and the same. God has revealed to Pharaoh what he is about to do . . . the seven worthless heads of grain scorched by the east wind: They are seven years of famine.'"

Genesis 41:25-27

"So they put slave masters over them to oppress them with forced labor, and they built Pithom and Rameses as store cities for Pharaoh. But the more they were oppressed, the more they multiplied and spread; so the Egyptians . . . made their lives bitter with hard labor . . . ."   Exodus 1:11-14

THE CHAIN OF ISRAEL

Gather Up: Several different colors of 9" x 12" construction paper, scissors, glue, tape, stapler

Get Ready: Cut the colored paper into 9-inch strips.

Go: Let children create colorful paper chains to remind them of two things: how the Hebrews served as slaves in Egypt, and how they grew and multiplied as a people. Children may use whatever means is easiest to connect the chains—stapling, gluing, or taping. Connect all the chains together and use them to decorate the room.

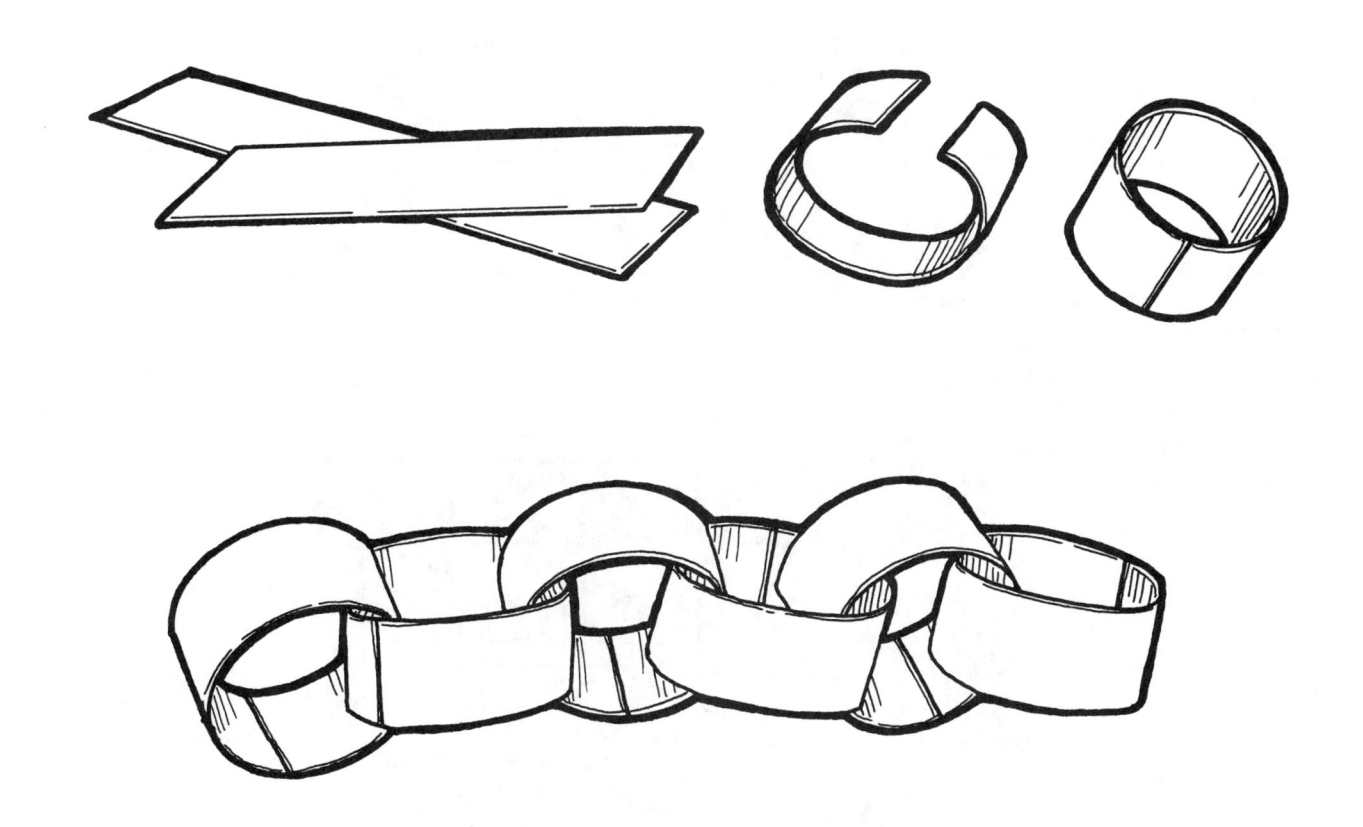

MOSES, MOSES GENTLY DOWN THE NILE

Gather Up: Pattern, strawberry baskets, dried leaves and grasses, cotton balls, brown construction paper, crayons, scissors, glue

Get Ready: If necessary, cut out the pattern and a piece of construction paper about the size of the pattern for each child.

Go: Have children fill their baskets with some dried leaves and grasses. Then let them color the pattern of baby Moses, cut it out, and glue it to construction paper. They may place baby Moses in their baskets with a few shredded cotton balls placed lightly on top to keep him warm.

(Sing to the tune of "Row, Row, Row Your Boat.")

Float, float, floating Moses,
Gently down the Nile.
Happily, happily, happily, happily,
Sleeping all the while!

"Then a new king, who did not know about Joseph, came to power in Egypt. 'Look,' he said to his people, 'the Israelites have become much too numerous for us.'"

Exodus 1:8-9

"Then Pharaoh gave this order to all his people: 'Every boy that is born you must throw into the Nile . . . .'"

Exodus 1:22

"and she became pregnant and gave birth to a son . . . . she got a papyrus basket for him . . . . and put it among the reeds along the bank of the Nile. Then Pharaoh's daughter went down to the Nile to bathe . . . . She saw the basket among the reeds and sent her slave girl to get it . . . . She named him Moses, saying, 'I drew him out of the water.'"

Exodus 2:2, 3, 5, 10

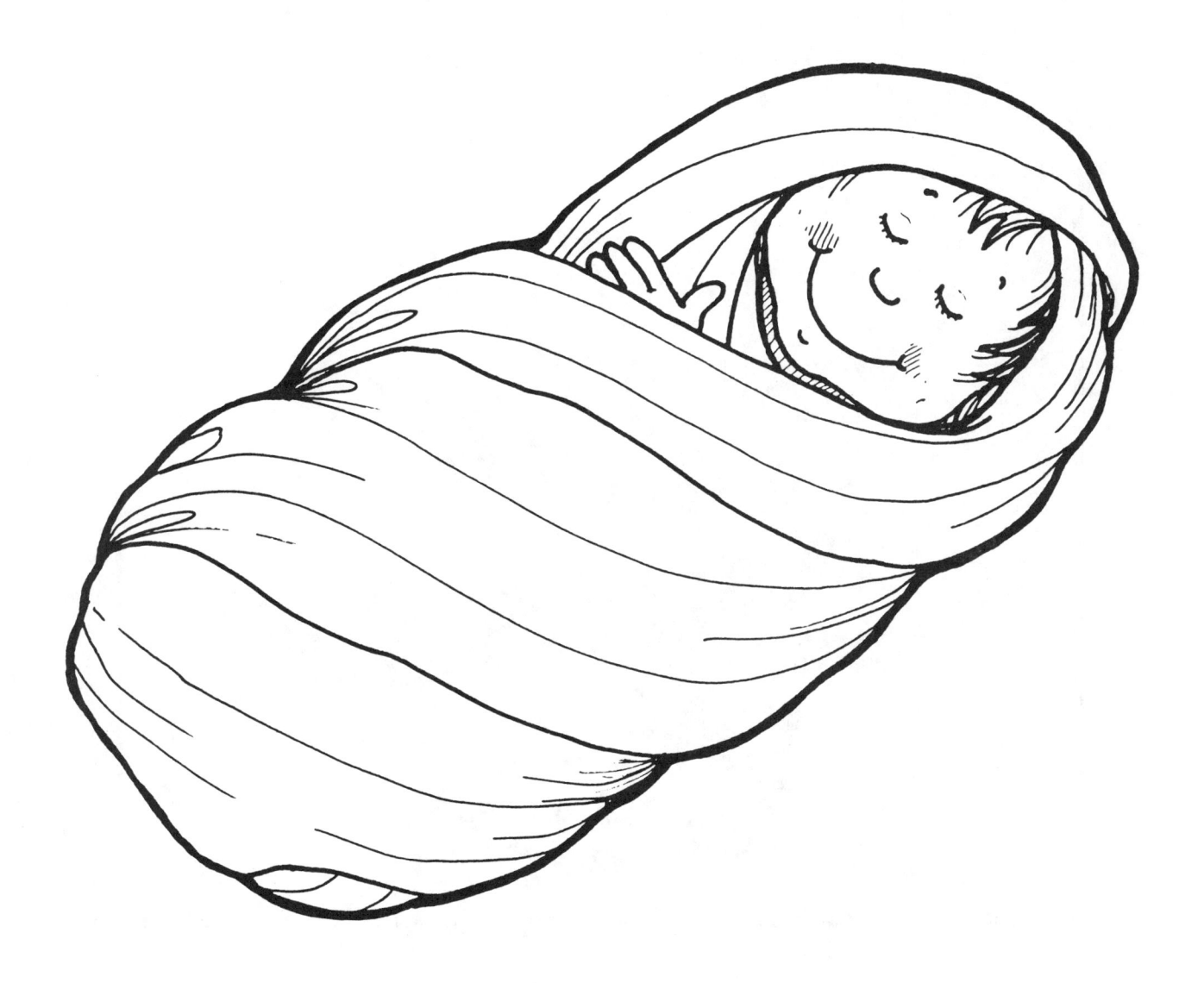

"There the angel of the Lord appeared to him in flames of fire from within a bush. Moses saw that though the bush was on fire it did not burn up." Exodus 3:2

THE BURNING BUSH

Gather Up: Sheets of white paper, red paper, green crayon, scissors, glue

Get Ready: Cut the red paper into small flame shapes.

Go: Help children trace around their hands on white paper with green crayon. Let them color the hand shapes with green crayon. Each hand is a bush! Children may drop spots of glue all over their hand shapes and press on red flames. Each child will have a burning bush for a reminder of how the Lord spoke to Moses.

"Then Moses stretched out his hand over the sea, and all that night the Lord drove the sea back with a strong east wind and turned it into dry land. The waters were divided"

Exodus 14:21

THE SEA DIVIDES

Gather Up: Sheets of plain white paper, blue tissue paper, brown crayon, sand or fine dirt, scissors, glue, brushes

Get Ready: Fold a sheet of paper in half for each child. Cut the tissue paper into strips.

Go: Have the child open the paper, color a wide strip of brown down the middle, and brush glue on either side of it. The tissue paper strips may then be pressed onto the glue to make the parting sea. A second layer of glue and tissue paper may be added if desired. Then help the child spread some glue on the brown-colored area and sprinkle some sand or fine dirt on it to show the dry path across the sea. Let dry. Children may close, then open their papers to see the great sea divide.

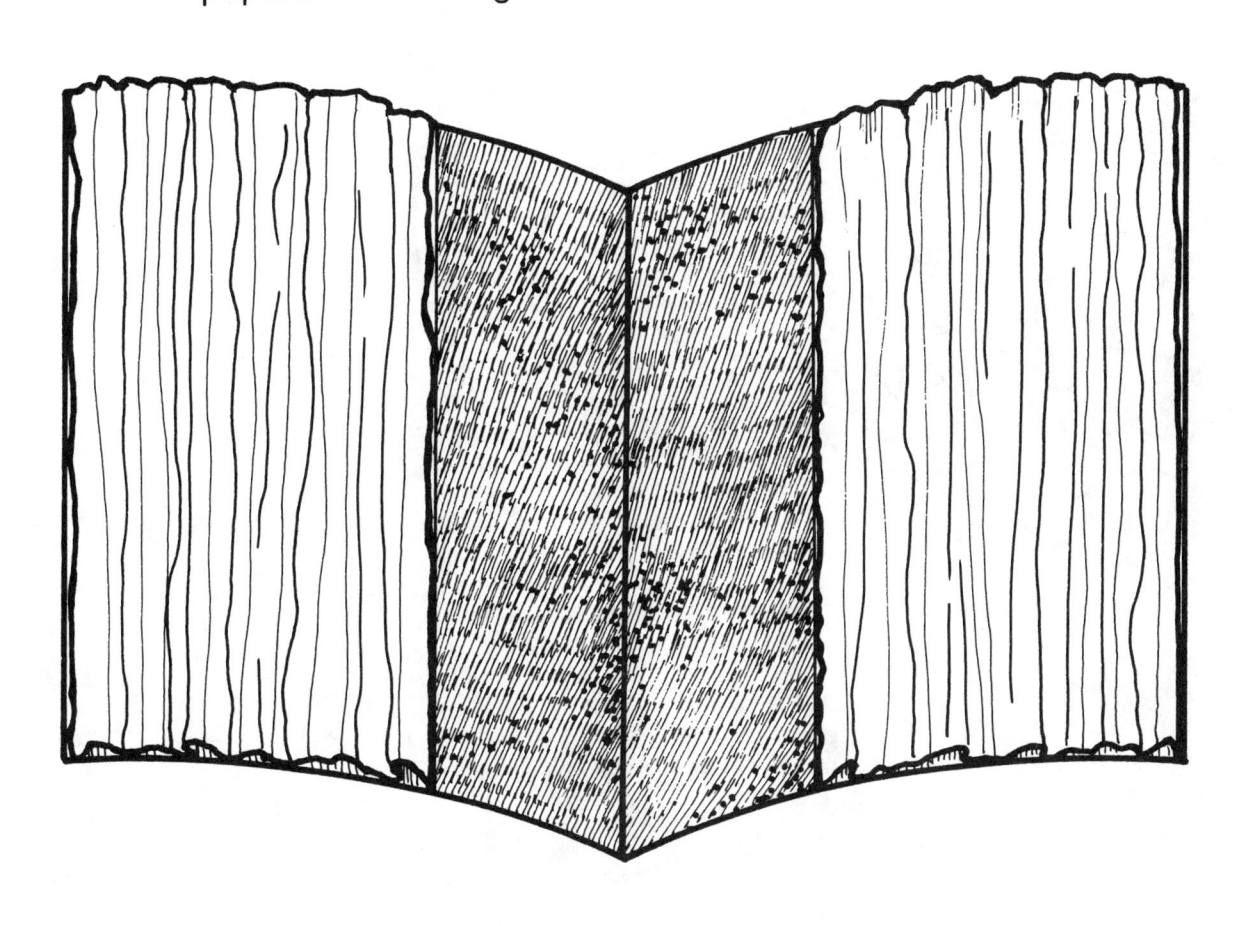

"... and the sound of the trumpet grew louder and louder. Then Moses spoke and the voice of God answered him. The Lord descended to the top of Mount Sinai and called Moses . . . . So Moses went up" Exodus 19:19-20

THE TRUMPET SOUNDS!

Gather Up: Paper towel tubes, two colors of crepe paper streamers, glitter, glue, newspaper

Get Ready: Cover a work table with newspaper. Cut about three 24" crepe paper streamers for each child.

Go: Have children spread glue around one end of the tubes, about a third of the way up. Then they can press on the streamers, letting them hang down from the tubes on either side. Let children decorate the tubes by spreading or dribbling glue in squiggly lines and swirls, and adding glitter to coat them. Have students hold the tubes over newspaper to avoid a mess. Set the trumpets on end to dry. Let children "play" their trumpets!

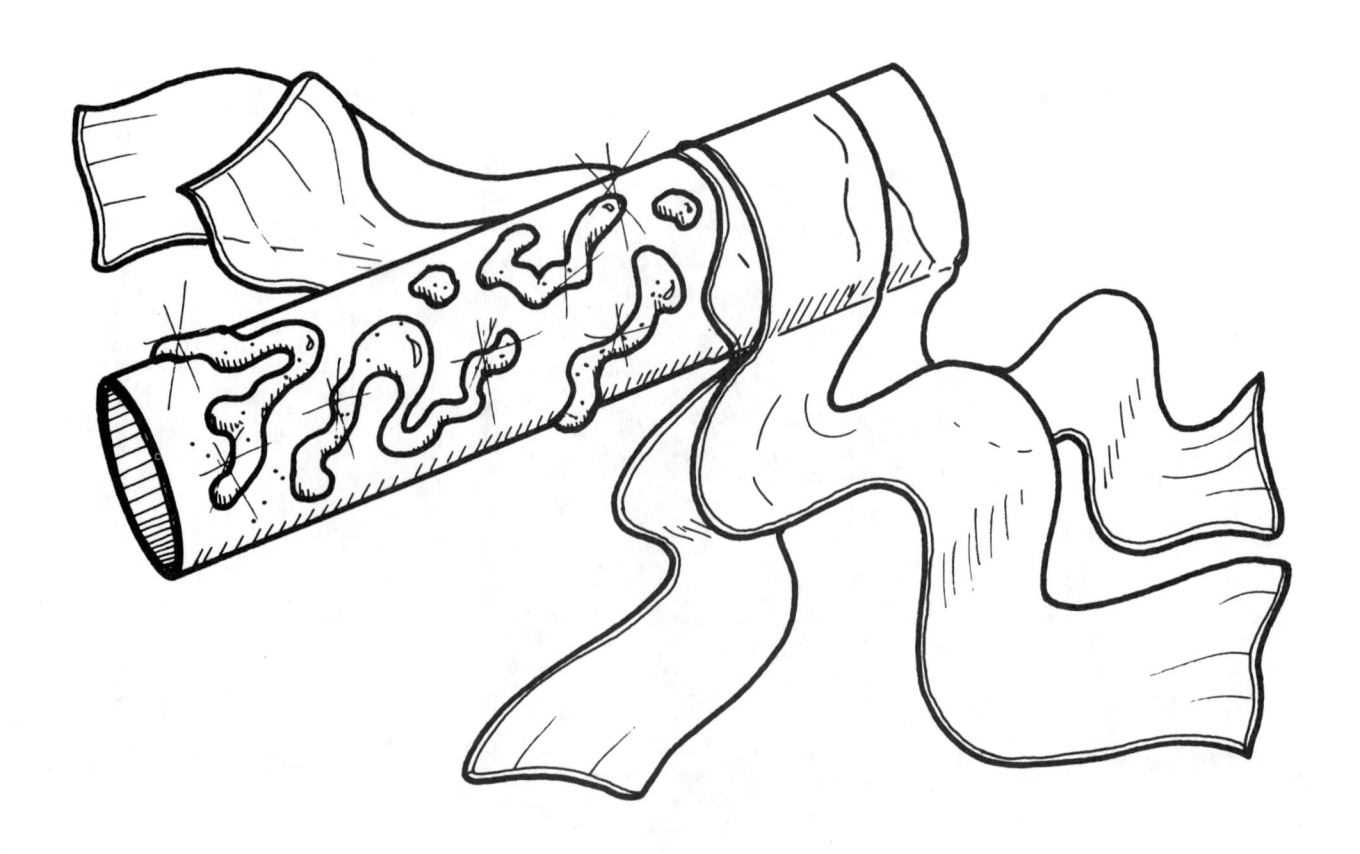

THE TEN COMMANDMENTS

Gather Up: Sheets of 12" x 18" brown construction paper, patterns, crayons, scissors, glue

Get Ready: Fold the paper in half. With the scissors, round off the top, starting at the right corner and ending at the left, so that the unfolded paper looks like two stone tablets.

Go: Let children color the two stone tablet patterns. Then let them try tracing over the dotted lines to make the numbers from one to ten. Have each child glue the first tablet on the left side of his brown paper, and the second tablet on the right.

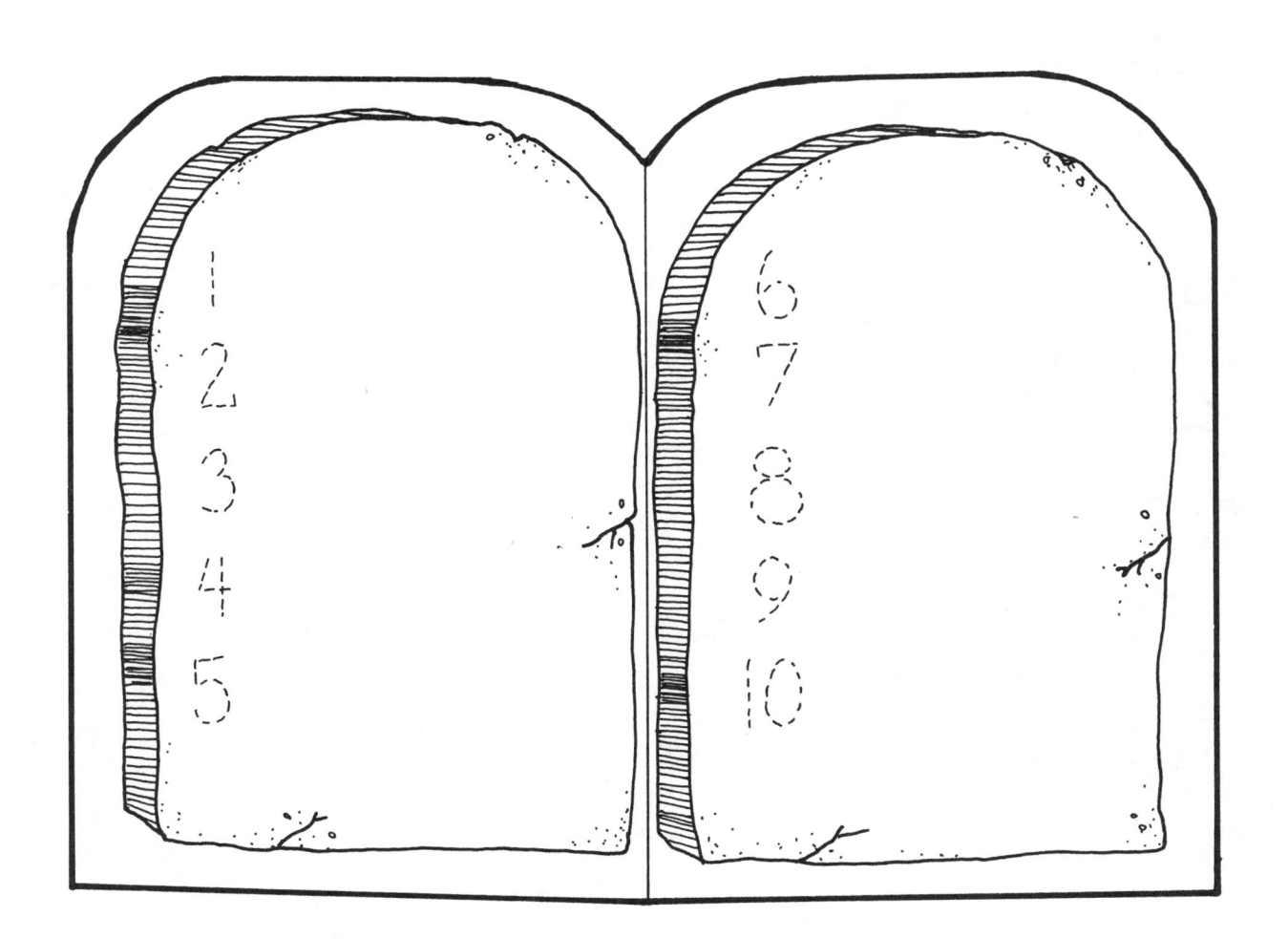

"And God spoke all these words: 'I am the Lord your God, who brought you out of Egypt, out of the land of slavery.'"
Exodus 20:1-2

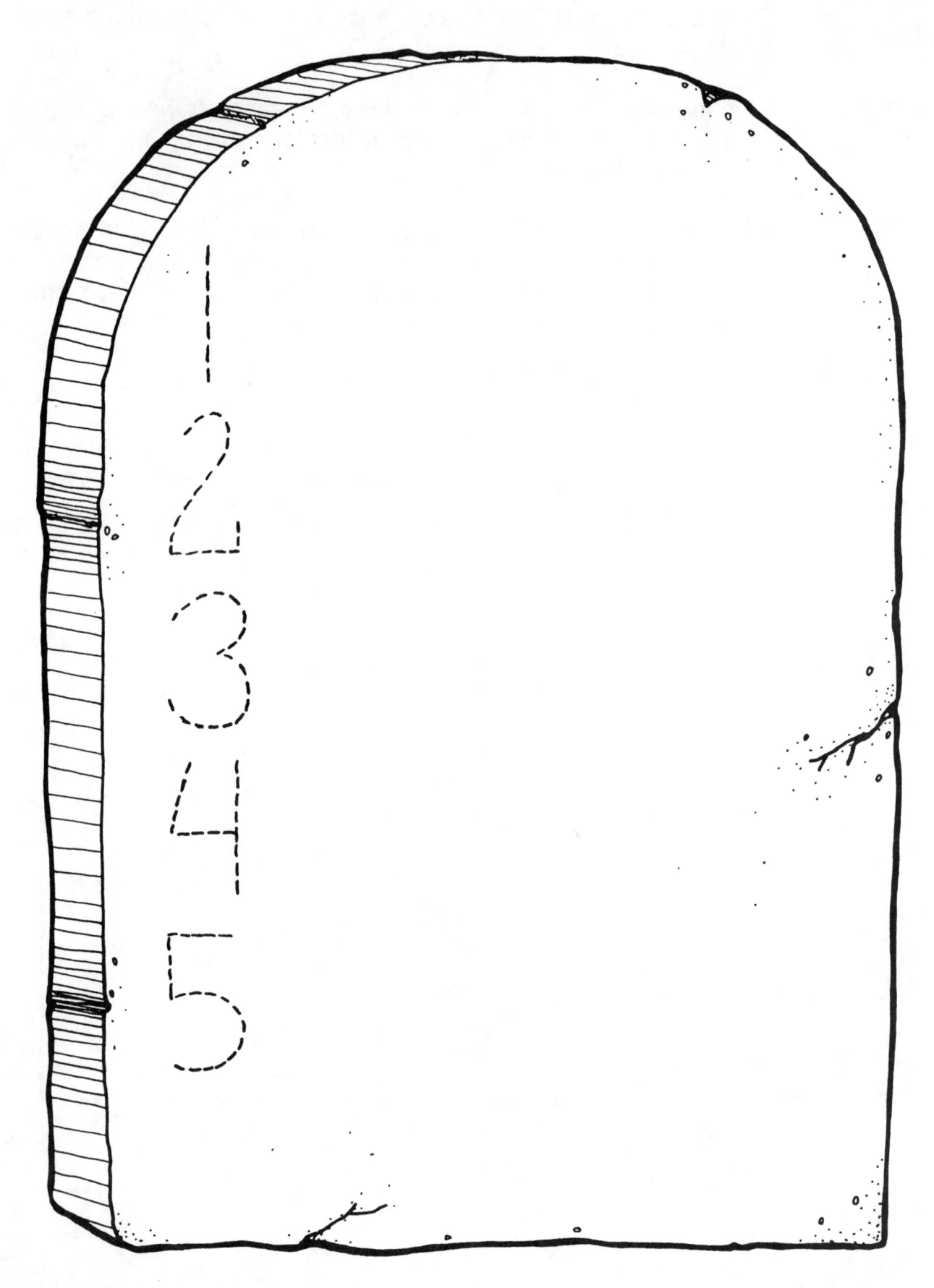

"Then the Lord said to Moses, 'Tell the Israelites this: You have seen for yourselves that I have spoken to you from heaven:'"   Exodus 20:22

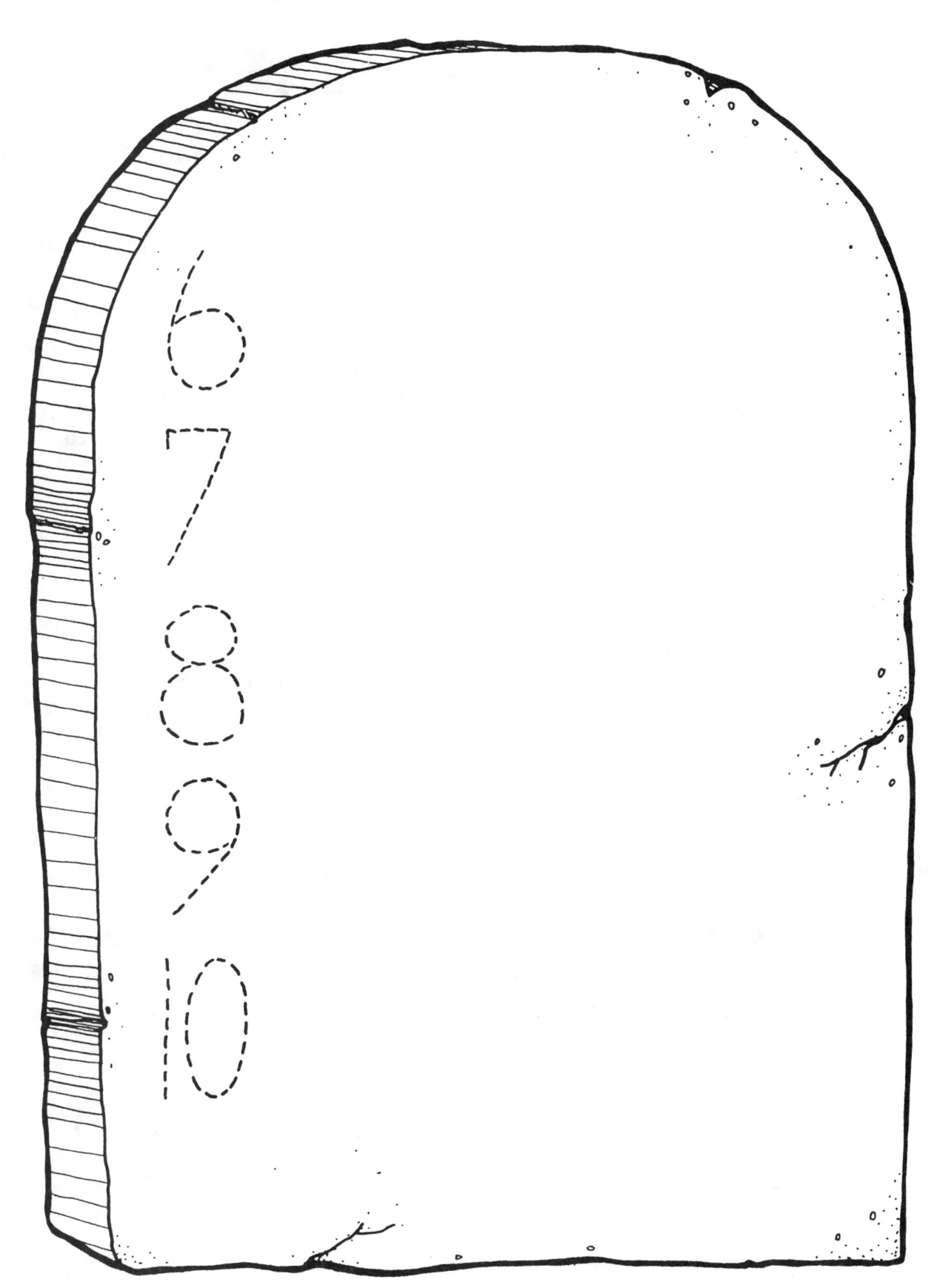

"So Moses went down to the people and told them." Exodus 19:25

FROM THE HEART
A COMMANDMENT COLLAGE

Gather Up: 12" x 18" sheets of red construction paper or one long strip of butcher paper or newsprint, old magazines, stickers, crayons, ribbons, scissors, glue

Get Ready: Decide whether the children will be making individual collages or a group project. For individual collages, cut a large heart from the red paper for each child. For a group project, mount a giant paper strip on a wall or chalkboard and cut smaller red hearts for children, just big enough to write their names on.

Go: Let children cut pictures from magazines to illustrate what makes them happy and reminds them to be loving and caring: families living and working together in harmony; people who help others, such as police officers, doctors, nurses, and teachers; children playing together. Each child may glue pictures randomly on an individual large heart or on the giant paper strip. Stickers, ribbons, and the child's own cheerful crayon drawings may also be added. Label each individual heart collage with the child's name, or have children write their names on the small hearts; glue these to the group collage. Then stand back and admire your work!

Note: Talk about the Ten Commandments before beginning. Ask children what they think the commands mean. Allow them to offer their ideas about how the Lord would like them to live their lives. Tell them that they will be making a collage celebrating the gifts of life and the goodness of giving and caring.

THE LAND OF MILK AND HONEY

Gather Up: Purple powdered tempera paint, baby powder, jumbo white cotton balls, sheets of 9" x 12" colored construction paper, pattern, small paper bag, newspaper, crayons, glue, scissors

Get Ready: Cover a work area with newspaper. Copy and cut out the number of patterns needed for your group. Pass out ten cotton balls and the other materials to each child. Place about a tablespoon of paint and a bit of baby powder in the bag; shake to mix.

Go: Let each child drop a few cotton balls at a time into the bag; then shake to color the cotton. Demonstrate how to take out the cotton balls and shake off the excess over the newspaper. Let children color all the balls. (Refill the bag with paint and powder as needed.)

Have each child color the stem and leaves of the pattern. Then let her choose a color of construction paper and glue the pattern to it. To complete the craft, the child glues each colored cotton ball to a circle to create a huge, ripe, bunch of grapes!

"When they reached the Valley . . . they cut off a branch bearing a single cluster of grapes. Two of them carried it on a pole between them . . . ."   Numbers 13:23

"They gave Moses this account: 'We went into the land to which you sent us, and it does flow with milk and honey! Here is its fruit.'" Numbers 13:27

A FEAST OF MILK AND HONEY

Gather Up: Sandwich bread, squeezable containers of honey, metal cookie cutters (heart and star shapes work well), plastic knives, paper cups, paper plates, milk

Get Ready: Get ready to share a feast together! Lay out bread slices on a work surface.

Go: Let children put a plate, a cup, and a knife at each child's place. Show them how to create special open-faced sandwiches by pressing quickly and firmly into the center of the bread with a cookie cutter. At the table they can squeeze a bit of honey onto their bread and spread it with plastic knives. Pour the milk, and let children share a sweet feast of milk and honey!

THE SUN STOOD STILL

Gather Up: White paper plates, yellow or orange copy paper, crayons, red, yellow, or orange ribbon, scissors, glue, hole punch

Get Ready: Make a copy of the pattern on colored paper for each child. Cut the ribbon into $2\frac{1}{2}$" to 3" pieces.

Go: Let children color the bright, glaring sun. Have them cover the centers of their paper plates with glue. Then they may glue the short pieces of ribbon all around the rim of the paper plates. Help them press the sun patterns onto the glue, catching the ends of the ribbons under the sun. When each sun is dry, punch a hole at the top and string with yarn to hang.

"... The sun stopped in the middle of the sky and delayed going down about a full day. There has never been a day like it before or since .... Surely the Lord was fighting for Israel!" Joshua 10:13-14

CHARIOTS OF IRON

Gather Up: Wheel-shaped macaroni, 9" x 12" colored construction paper, pattern, crayons, scissors, glue, yarn, hole punch

Get Ready: Make a copy of the pattern for each child. If necessary, cut it out.

Go: If children want to, they may color their chariot wheels. Then let them glue wheel-shaped macaroni all around the paper wheels. When the wheels are dry, they may be glued to sturdy construction paper. Punch a hole on either side of the wheel, and string with yarn to hang.

"... The commander of his army was Sisera ... he had nine hundred iron chariots and had cruelly oppressed the Israelites ... they cried to the Lord for help."

Judges 4:2-3

"Then Deborah said ... 'Go! This is the day the Lord has given Sisera into your hands.' ... the Lord routed Sisera and all his chariots ... Sisera abandoned his chariot and fled on foot."

Judges 4:14-15

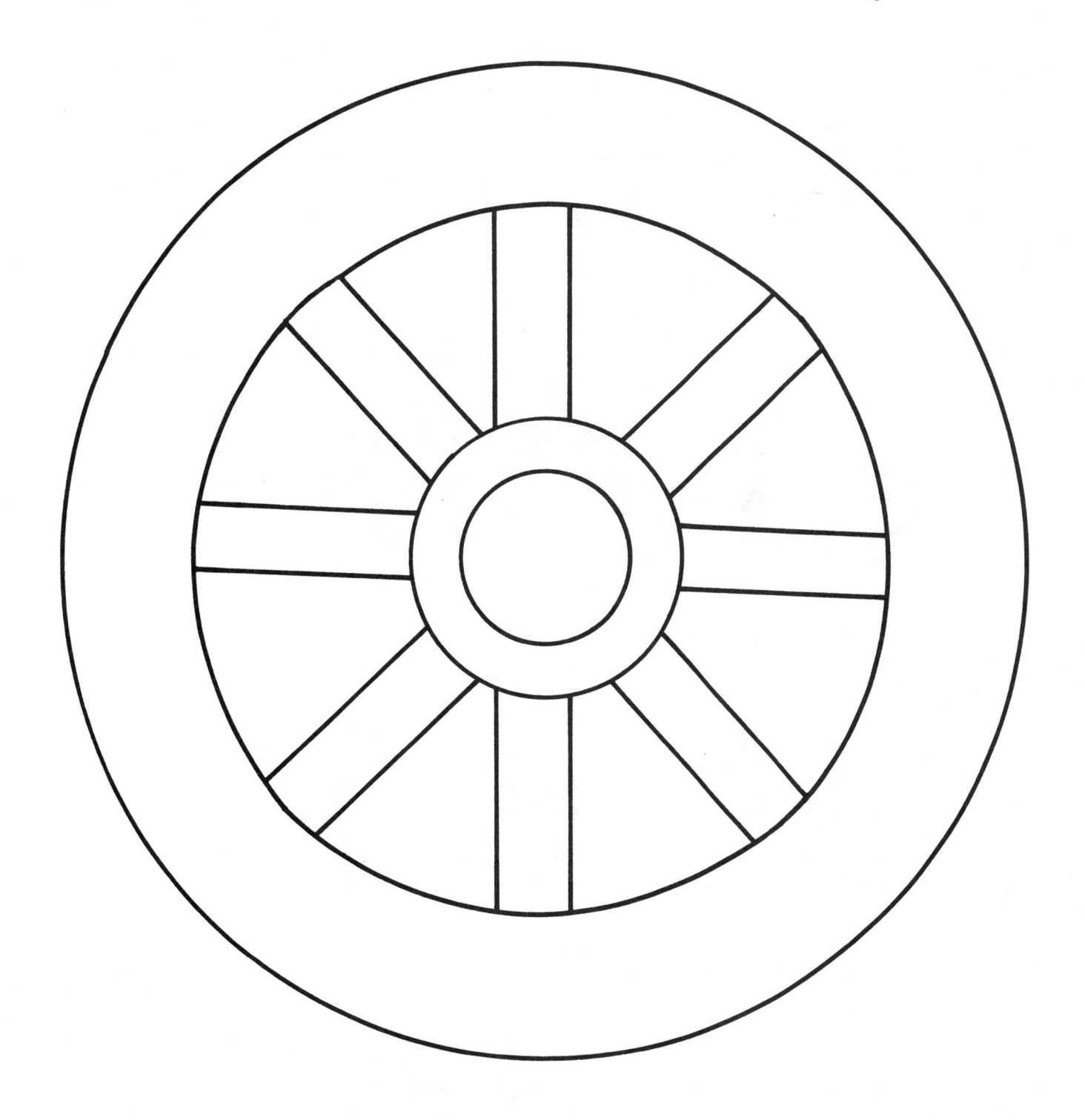

SAMSON

Gather Up: Rye grass seed (inexpensive and available in bulk at most feed and seed stores), large paper cups, potting soil, pattern, crayons, scissors, glue, pencil

Get Ready: Make a copy of the pattern for each child. Poke a few small pencil holes in the bottoms of the cups for drainage.

Go: Let children color their Samson patterns and then glue them to the front of their cups. They may fill their cups with potting soil, sprinkle in some seed, and lightly cover the seed with soil. Let children put their cups in the sun, and water only enough to keep the soil moist, being careful not to dislodge the seeds. In about two weeks, they can watch the mighty Samson's hair grow!

"... you will conceive and give birth to a son. No razor may be used on his head, because the boy is to be a Nazirite, set apart to God from birth, and he will begin the deliverance of Israel from the hands of the Philistines." Judges 13:5

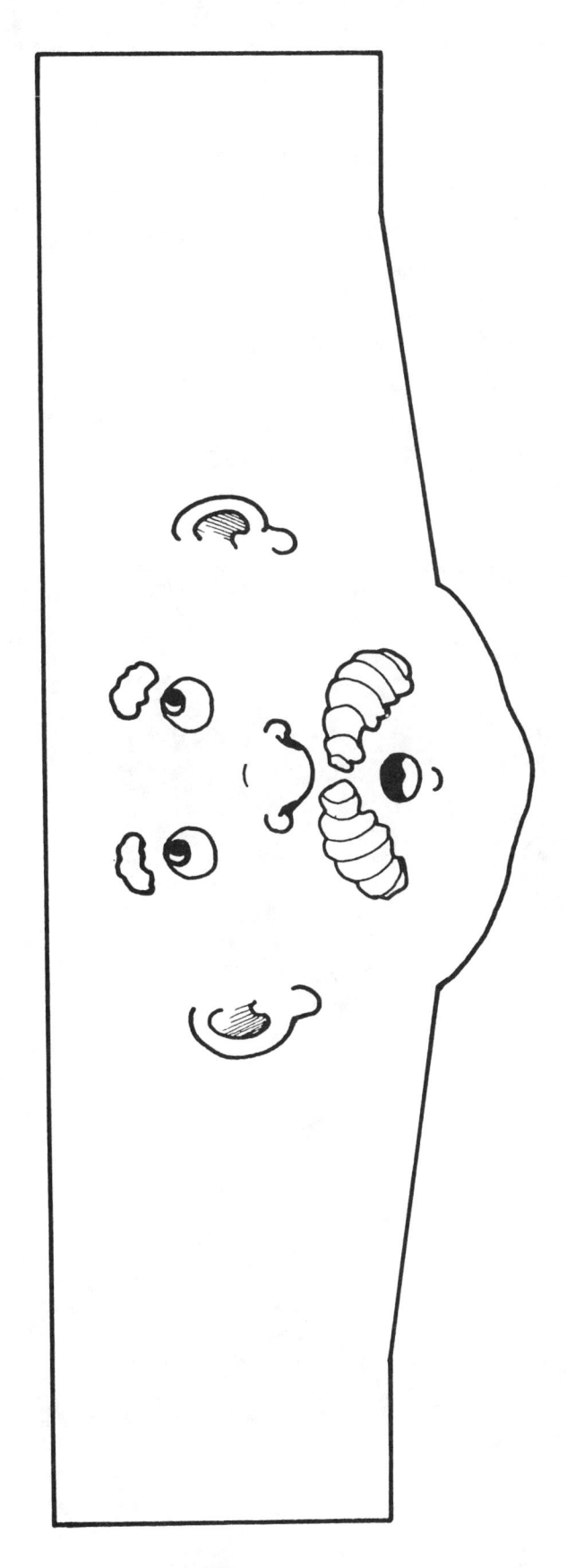

GIDEON
THE MIRACLE OF THE MESSENGER

Gather Up: Crackers, 9" x 12" sheets of black, red, orange, and yellow construction paper, patterns, crayons, scissors, glue

Get Ready: Use the patterns to cut flame shapes from red, orange, and yellow construction paper.

Go: Let children glue the bright flames to the center of the black paper. They may glue a few crackers at the bottom of the flames to represent the unleavened cakes that were consumed by fire when the angel appeared to Gideon.

"With the tip of the staff that was in his hand, the angel of the Lord touched the meat and the unleavened bread. Fire flared . . . . And the angel of the Lord disappeared. When Gideon realized that it was the angel of the Lord, he exclaimed, 'Ah, Sovereign Lord! . . .'" Judges 6:21-22

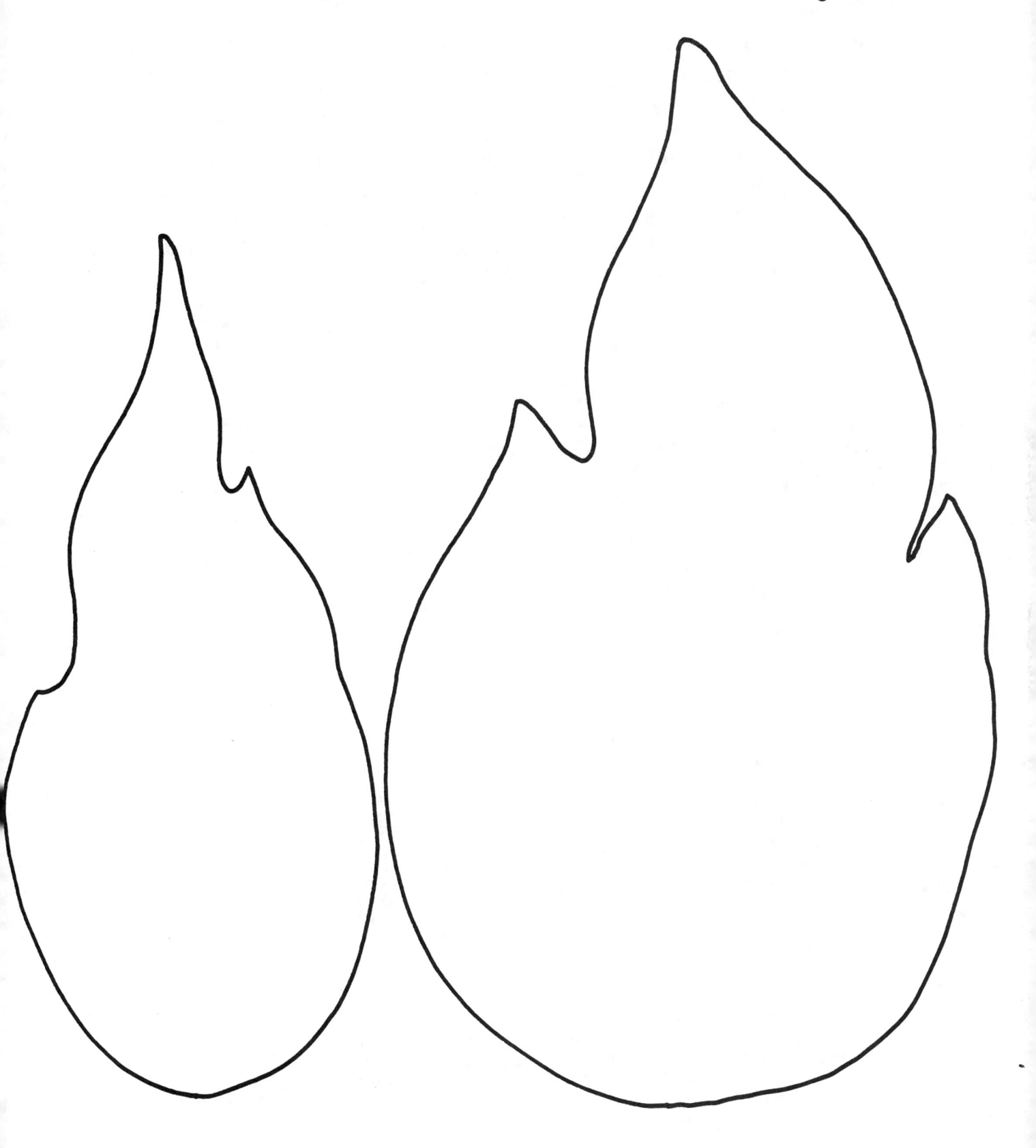

THE DEW ON THE FLEECE

Gather Up: Large white cotton balls, brown construction paper, pattern, scissors, brushes, glue, hole punch, yarn

Get Ready: Copy the pattern and cut one out for each child. Cut brown construction paper into background shapes a little larger than the pattern.

Go: Have children pull on the cotton balls to make them light and fluffy. They may glue the fleece shape to the brown paper background, brush glue all over the fleece shape, and press fluffy cotton onto it to make a thick fleece. When dry, punch two holes at the top corners, and string with yarn to hang.

"Then Gideon said to God . . . 'Allow me one more test with the fleece. This time make the fleece dry and the ground covered with dew.' That night God did so. Only the fleece was dry; all the ground was covered with dew."   Judges 6:39-40

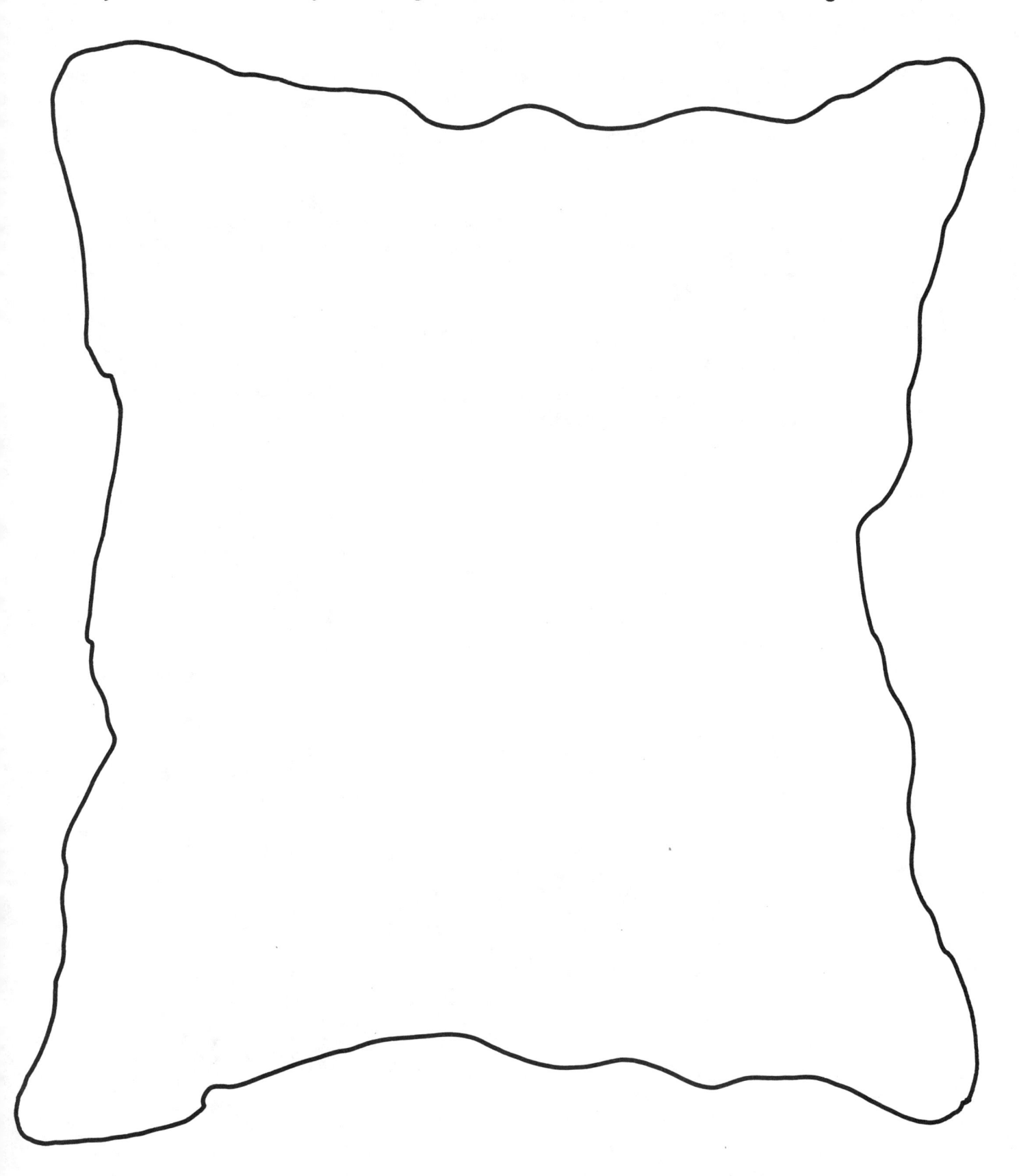

DAVID AND GOLIATH

Gather Up: Egg cartons, craft sticks, paper towel tubes, beans, crayons, scissors, glue

Get Ready: Cut out one egg cup from the carton for each child. Copy the pattern and cut one out for each child. Cut about 2 or 3 inches off the tube to make it shorter. Be sure to cut evenly so the tube will stand up.

Go: Help children make David's slingshot by gluing the end of a craft stick to the back of an egg cup. Place these in a low-heat oven to dry quickly.

Have each child color the picture of Goliath; then glue it around the tube. Set Goliath on a tabletop. Show children how to put a bean in the cup, hold the sling back, and sling the bean toward Goliath to knock him down. Supervise this activity carefully.

"Reaching into his bag and taking out a stone, he slung it and struck the Philistine on the forehead. The stone sank into his forehead, and he fell facedown on the ground."

I Samuel 17:49

JONAH'S WHALE OF A TIME

Gather Up: Sheets of 12" x 18" blue construction paper, patterns, crayons, scissors, glue

Get Ready: Make a copy of the Jonah pattern for each child. Fold the blue paper in half. Place the bottom of the whale pattern along the fold of the paper and outline. Make a whale for each child. Let children cut out the whales or do this for them.

Go: Let each child draw an eye and a smile on the whale. Then color the figure of Jonah, and glue him inside the whale.

"But the Lord provided a great fish to swallow Jonah, and Jonah was inside the fish three days and three nights."   Jonah 1:17

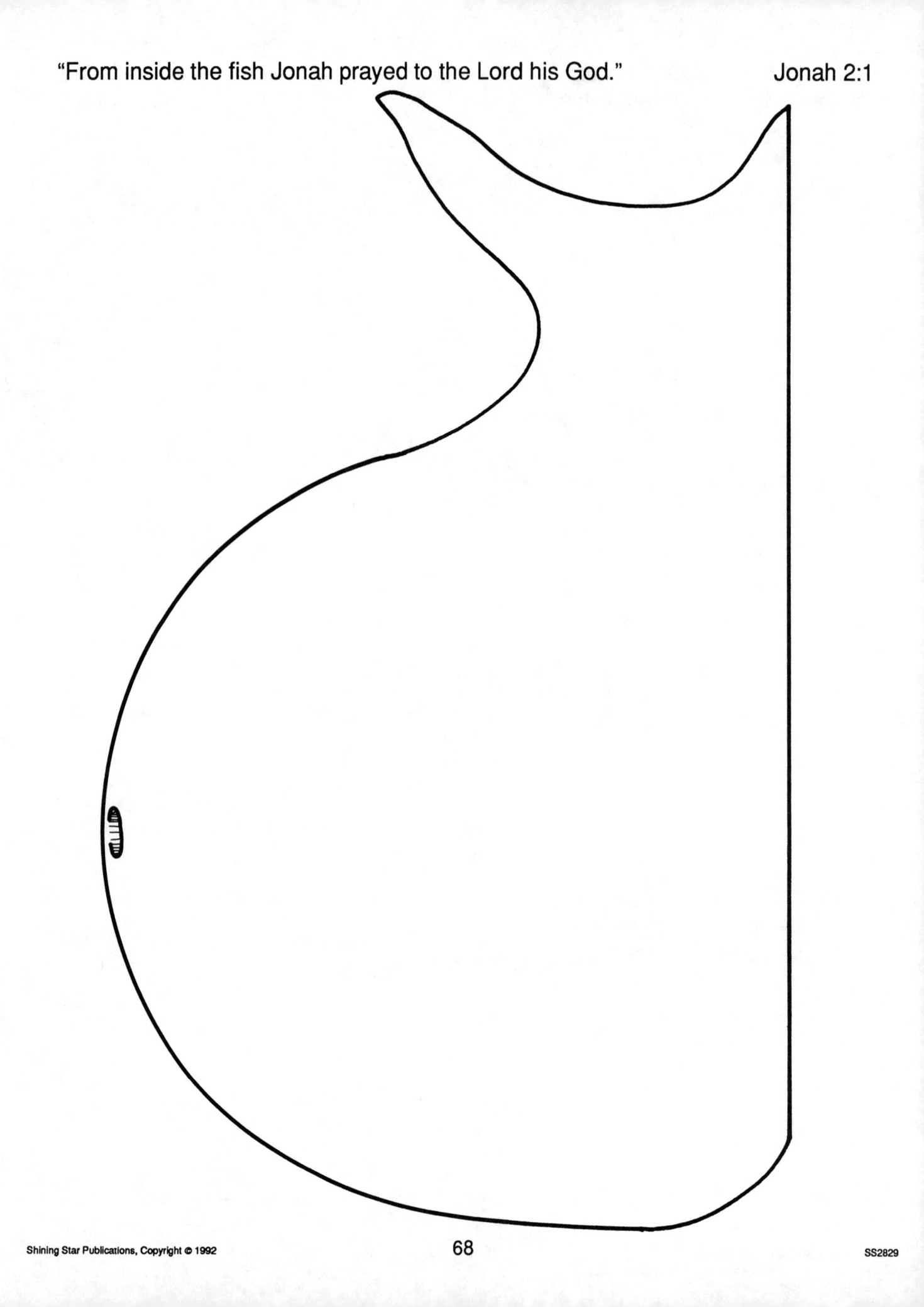

"From inside the fish Jonah prayed to the Lord his God."   Jonah 2:1

"But the angel said to her, 'Do not be afraid, Mary, you have found favor with God. You will be with child and give birth to a son, and you are to give him the name Jesus.'" Luke 1:30-31

GABRIEL VISITS MARY

Gather Up: Lollipops, yellow or white paper napkins, yellow, gold, or silver pipe cleaners, curly hair and small googly eyes (found in variety or craft stores), fine-point marker, glue

Get Ready: Put together a sample to show children before they begin.

Go: Show children how to unfold two paper napkins, lay them on top of each other, place a lollipop in the center, and gather the napkins around the stick. Twist a pipe cleaner around the stick to hold the napkins on. Fold back the ends of the pipe cleaner to make wings. Let children spread glue on the top and press on curly angel hair; then dab on two spots of glue and press on googly eyes. If they wish, they may draw smiles on their angels' faces. This angel craft is fun to make and fun to eat later!

TOOLS OF THE TRADE

Gather Up: Jumbo craft sticks (longer and wider than regular craft sticks), brown construction paper, patterns, scissors, glue

Get Ready: Cut a hammer and saw pattern from brown paper for each child.

Go: Each child should glue the blade pattern on a craft stick to make a saw. For the hammer, the child folds the pattern on the dotted line and coats half of it with glue. Then he places a craft stick in the middle and folds the hammerhead over it to glue it together.

Talk about the kinds of things Joseph might have made with his hammer and saw. Did Jesus learn how to use these tools? Ask children to share what they know about using hammers and saws and discuss who taught them.

"Isn't this the carpenter's son?" Matthew 13:55a

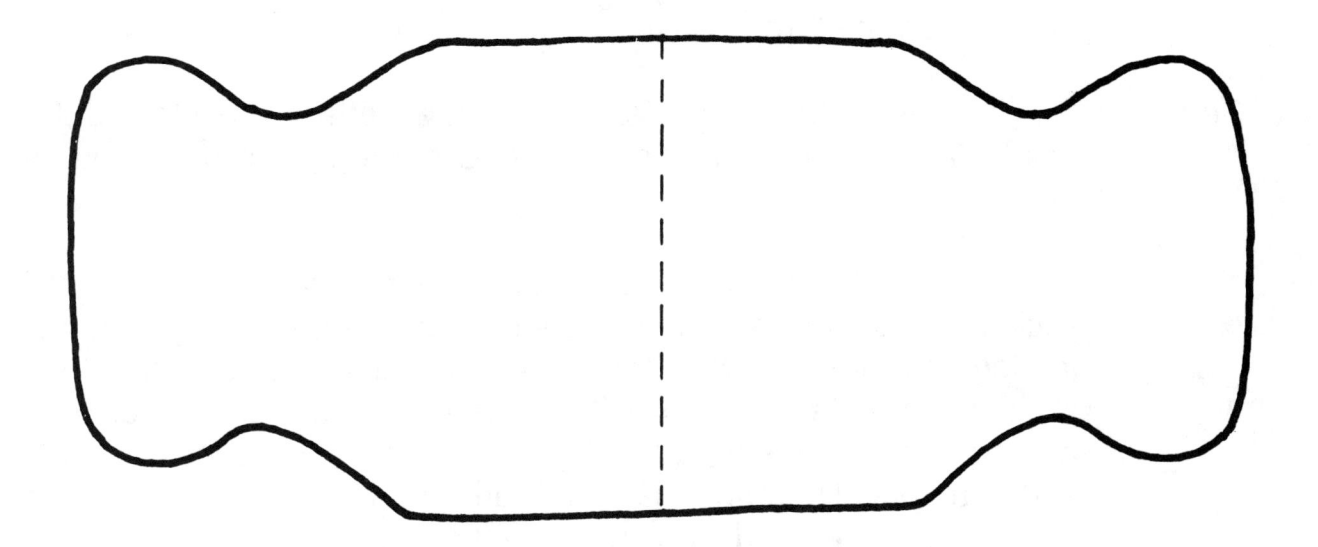

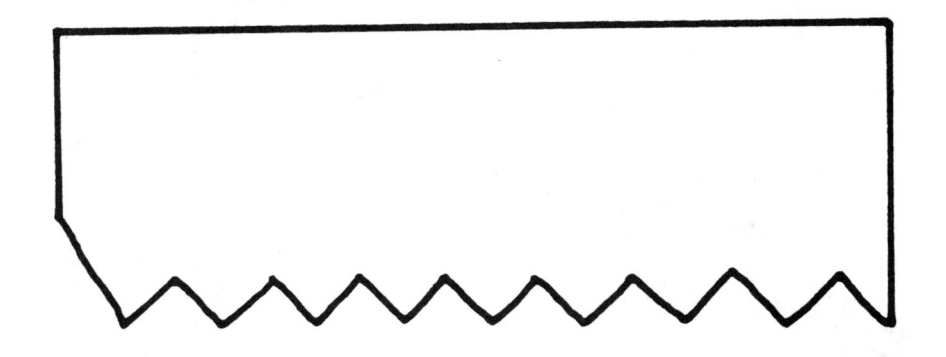

THE RIDE TO BETHLEHEM

Gather Up: Brown felt, brown pipe cleaners, 1" corks, jumbo craft sticks, brown paper, small googly eyes, black marker, scissors, hole punch, glue, pattern

Get Set: Cut felt pieces for all children, using the pattern provided. Cut a small piece of brown paper for ears. Cut the pipe cleaners into 4" lengths.

Go: Have each child coat one side of the felt piece with glue, place the stick in the center, and fold the felt in half around it, pressing the felt together firmly. This is the body of the donkey. (Enough of the stick should extend out on either side to provide for the donkey's face and for a handle.) The child may draw a black nose on the end of a cork. Then she may glue the ears to the back side of the top of the stick, and add two googly eyes and the cork nose. When the "donkey" is dry, punch a hole at the back end, poke a pipe cleaner through, and help the child twist it to make a tail.

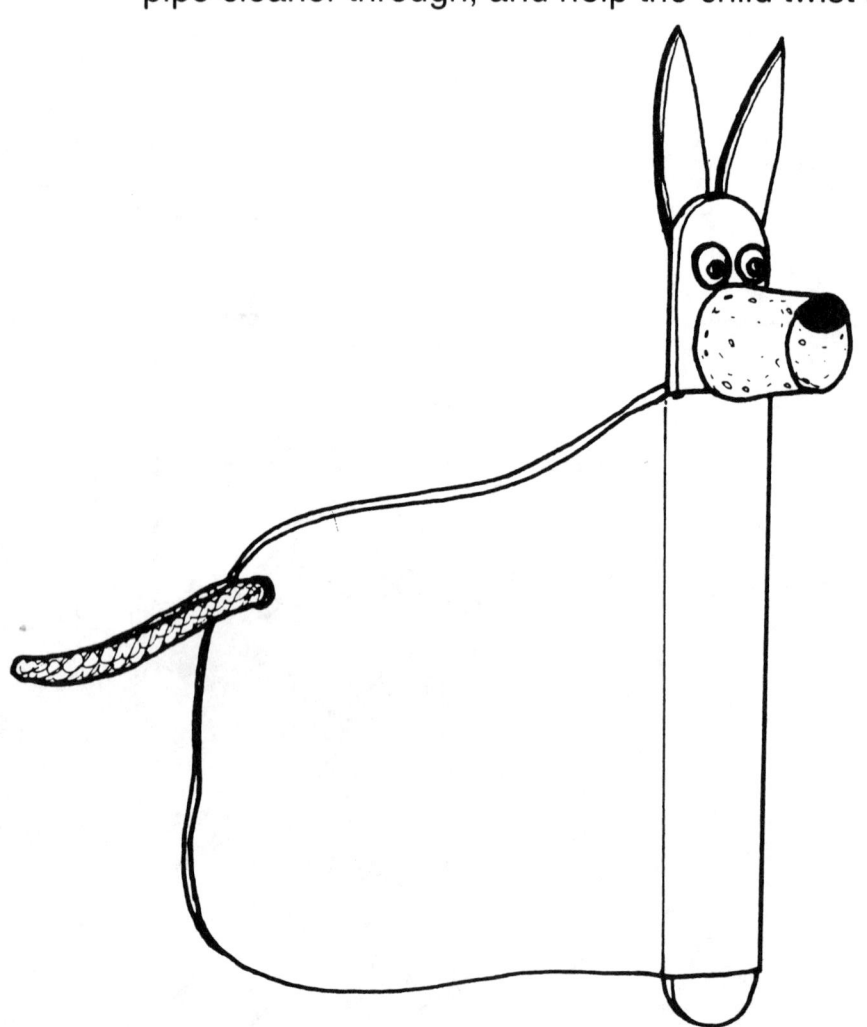

"So Joseph also went . . . to Bethlehem the town of David . . . to register with Mary, who was pledged to be married to him and was expecting a child."

Luke 2:4-5

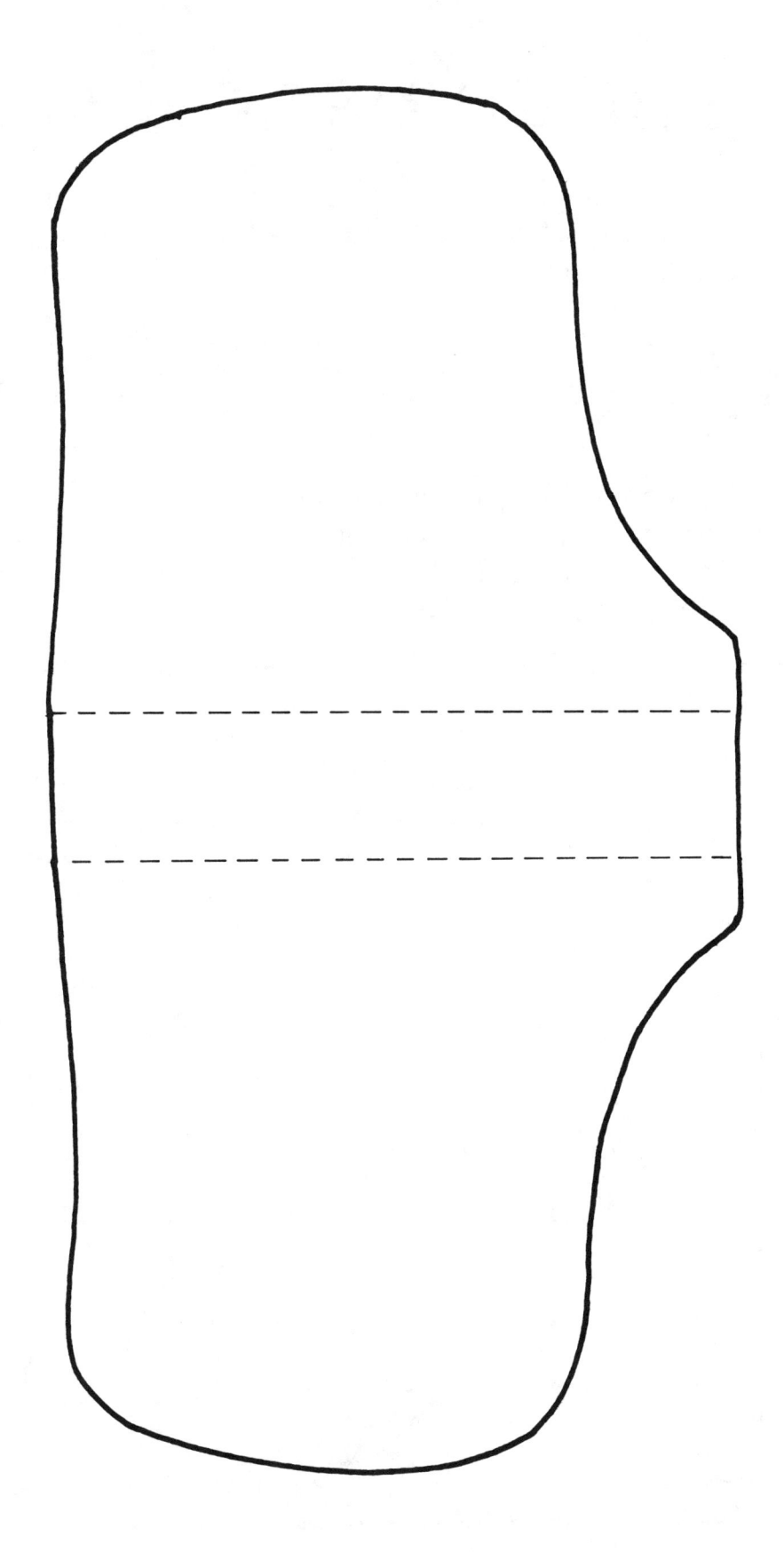

"and she gave birth to her firstborn, a son. She wrapped him in cloths and placed him in a manger, because there was no room for them in the inn."   Luke 2:7

THE CHRIST CHILD

Gather Up: 9" x 12" sheets of purple, red, or green construction paper, pink paper, craft sticks, large gold starburst sequins, cotton balls, pen, scissors, glue

Get Set: For each child, cut a circle from the pink paper about the size of a half dollar. Draw on it two eyes, a nose, and a smile, or let the child do this.

Go: On a sheet of construction paper, have each child glue four craft sticks to make the shape of a stable. Then he may glue the pink face and a few fluffed cotton balls for swaddling clothes inside the stable. A gold sequin above the stable becomes the star!

"After they had heard the king, they went on their way, and the star they had seen in the east went ahead of them until it stopped over the place where the child was."
Matthew 2:9

THREE WISE MEN

Get Ready: Patterns, crayons, markers, glitter, toilet tissue tubes, scissors, glue

Get Set: Copy the patterns of the wise men for each child. If necessary, cut them out for the children.

Go: Encourage children to do their best coloring to decorate the costumes of the three wise men. They may wish to add some glitter. Then they should spread the patterns with glue and press them around the tubes. These little stand-up hand puppets may be used by children to act out the Christmas story or make nativity scenes. Use the other crafts the children have made to complete the scenes.

"After Jesus was born in Bethlehem in Judea, during the time of King Herod, Magi from the east came to Jerusalem"

Matthew 2:1

. . . "Where is the one who has been born king of the Jews? We saw his star in the east and have come to worship him."

Matthew 2:2

"Then Herod called the Magi secretly and found out from them the exact time the star had appeared."

Matthew 2:7

"... The kingdom of heaven is like a mustard seed.... Though it is the smallest of all your seeds, yet when it grows, it is the largest of garden plants and becomes a tree, so that the birds of the air come and perch in its branches."

Matthew 13:31-32

THE MUSTARD SEED

Gather Up: 9" x 12" purple, brown, or black construction paper, whole mustard seeds (look in the spice section of the grocery store), green and yellow construction paper, glue

Get Ready: Help children tear green paper into long strips of varying lengths. Tear out small, rounded, odd shapes from the yellow paper for flowers.

Go: Let children glue the green strips for the stems and leaves of mustard plants on dark paper. They may glue the yellow flowers on the stems. Then spread glue on and around the flowers, and sprinkle whole mustard seeds to stick to the glue. Let dry completely.

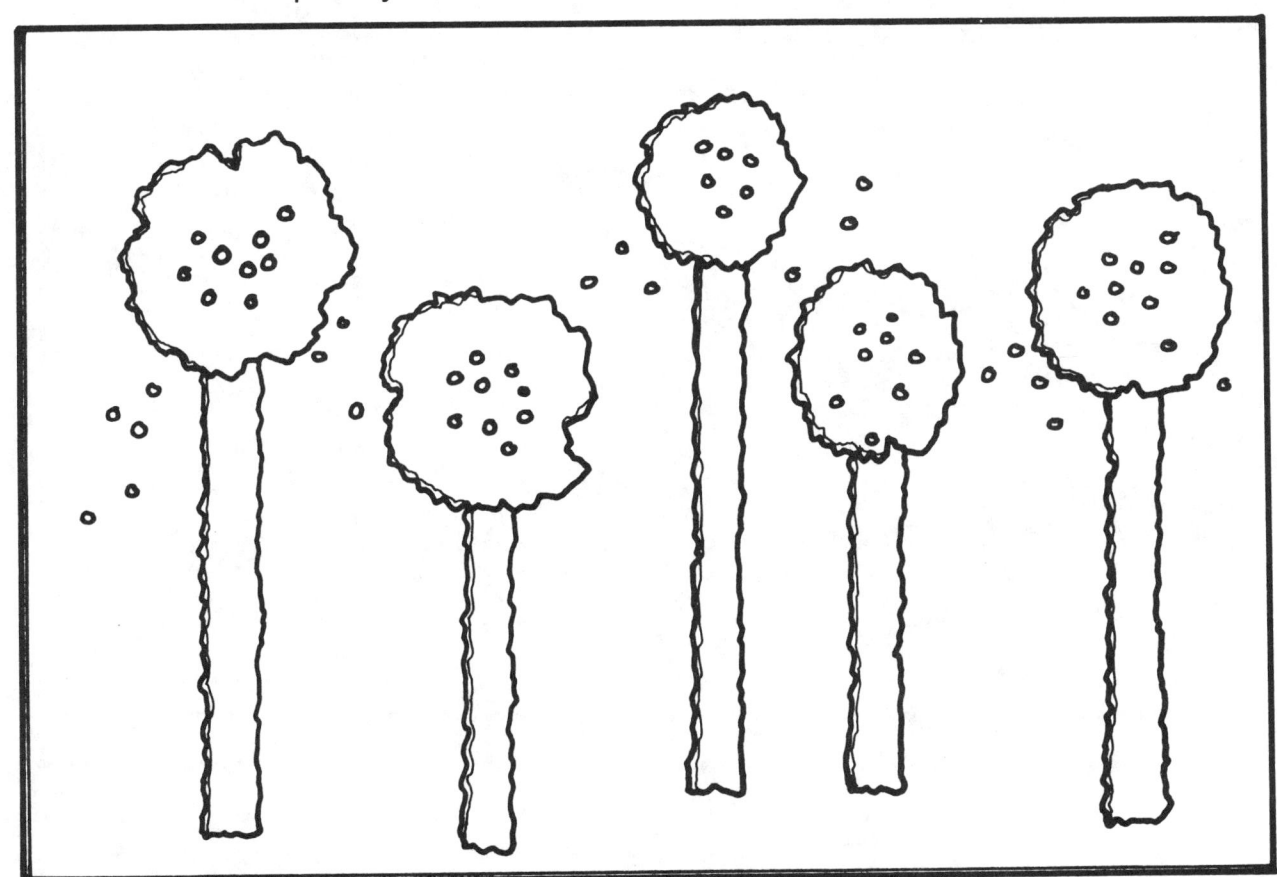

LITTLE FISH IN THE SEA

Gather Up: Strawberry baskets, 9" x 12" black construction paper, silver glitter, crayons or markers, scissors, glue

Get Ready: Copy the snail and fish patterns for each child. Cut the strawberry baskets into small flat sections.

Go: Let children use bright colors to color their fish; then glue them to black paper. Help them spread glue all around their fish, perhaps in seaweed shapes; then sprinkle glitter over the glue. Children may glue cut-up basket sections over portions of their pictures to represent fishing nets. Let dry completely.

"Once again, the kingdom of heaven is like a net that was let down into the lake and caught all kinds of fish. When it was full, the fishermen pulled it up on the shore. Then they sat down and collected the good fish in baskets, but threw the bad away. This is how it will be at the end of the age...." Matthew 13:47-49

LITTLE LOST LAMB

Gather Up: 9" x 12" colored construction paper, pattern, large cotton balls, paper bags, black powdered tempera paint, baby powder, crayons, scissors, glue, newspaper

Get Ready: Make copies of the lamb pattern for the children. If necessary, cut the patterns out for them. Cover a work area with newspaper. Put about a tablespoon of black powdered paint and a bit of baby powder in the paper bag. Shake it to mix. Color cotton balls (enough for your group) by dropping them into the bag and shaking it to coat them with paint. Shake off the excess over the newspaper. Supply some white cotton balls as well.

Go: Have children color the hooves and faces of their lambs if they wish. Then have them glue their lambs to colored paper backgrounds. Show them how to glue on cotton balls to complete their little lost lambs. They may make dusty black sheep, snowy white ones, or even spotted ones!

"... If a man owns a hundred sheep, and one of them wanders away, will he not leave ... and go to look for the one that wandered off? And if he finds it, I tell you the truth, he is happier about that one sheep than about the ninety-nine that did not wander off."

Matthew 18:12-13

"Here is a boy with five small barley loaves and two small fish, but how far will they go among so many? Jesus then took the loaves, gave thanks, and distributed to those who were seated as much as they wanted. He did the same with the fish."

John 6:9, 11

FEEDING FIVE THOUSAND

Gather Up: A fresh flat fish, craft paint, rice paper or other lightweight paper, paint brush, newspaper, spoon, dime

Get Ready: Try to buy a fairly large, whole fish with as flat a surface as possible. Lay it on the newspaper. Tuck under fins that may be sticking up. Place a dime over the eye so that it remains white and children can color it a bright contrasting color. Mix up the paint.

Go: Let children brush on paint to coat the fish. Do not paint the dime. If you've invested in rice paper, use some inexpensive paper to make "trial" prints. Carefully place the paper over the fish for the children. Let a child use a spoon to smooth the paper down over the fish. Then carefully peel back the paper to see the print. When the paint is dry, the eye can be painted a contrasting color.

Note: It's wise to practice a few times with different amounts of paint and different "spooning" techniques, but children will love the finished product!

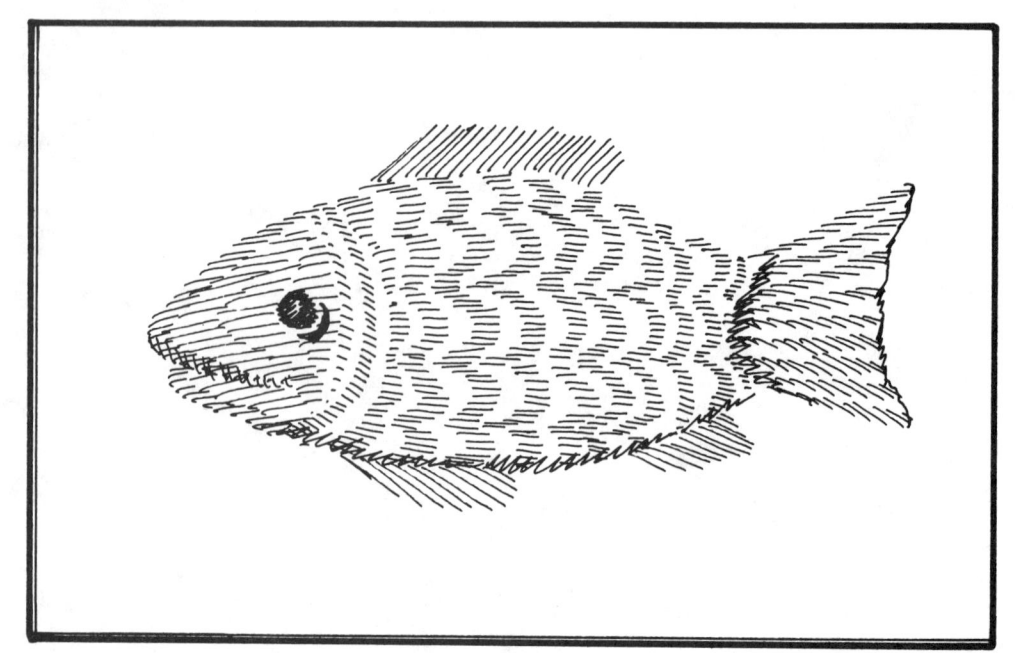

JESUS RIDES INTO JERUSALEM

Gather Up: Paper towel tubes, 9" x 12" green construction paper, gold glitter, scissors, glue, pattern

Get Ready: Fold the green paper in half, then in half again (see diagram). Follow the solid lines on the pattern to cut the paper into the shape of a large tree leaf. Notice the slits cut into one edge. Make one of these for each child.

Go: Let children unfold their leaves and spread glue over them in random patterns. They may sprinkle glitter on the glue to make sparkly fronds. When each child is done, slide the tube through the slits so he can wave his branch in the air as Jesus' followers did when He entered Jerusalem.

"A very large crowd spread their cloaks on the road, while others cut branches from the trees.... The crowds... shouted,... 'Blessed is he who comes in the name of the Lord! Hosanna in the highest!'"   Matthew 21:8-9

folded edge

cut →

cut →

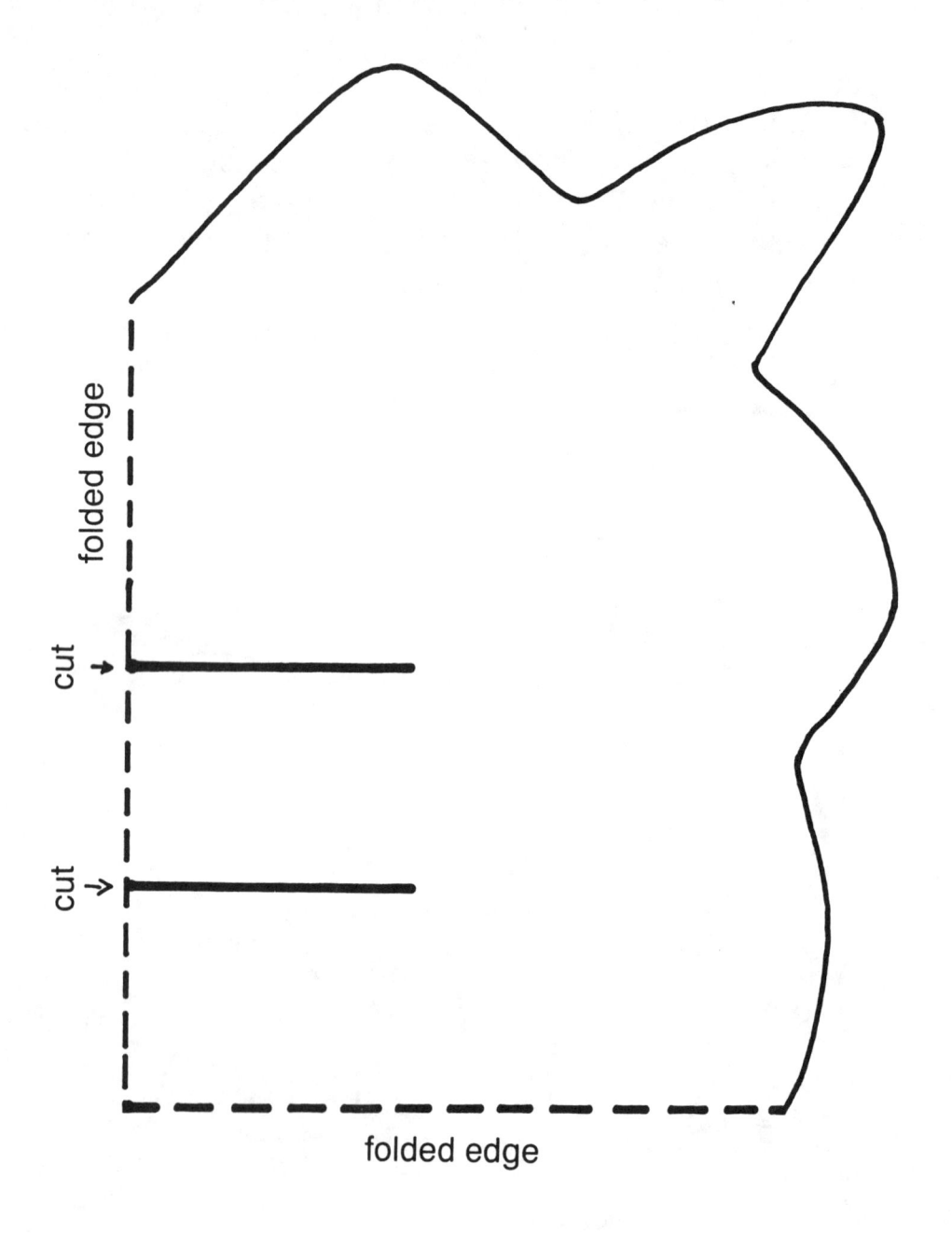

folded edge

THE LAST SUPPER

Gather Up: 9" x 12" yellow construction paper, crayons, pattern, scissors, glue

Get Ready: Make a copy of the two pattern pieces for each child. Cut them out for the children if necessary.

Go: Let the children color the grapes and bread. They may glue these to yellow construction paper to make special dinner place mats. Label each with the child's name. Encourage the children to use their place mats and share a special prayer with their families at suppertime.

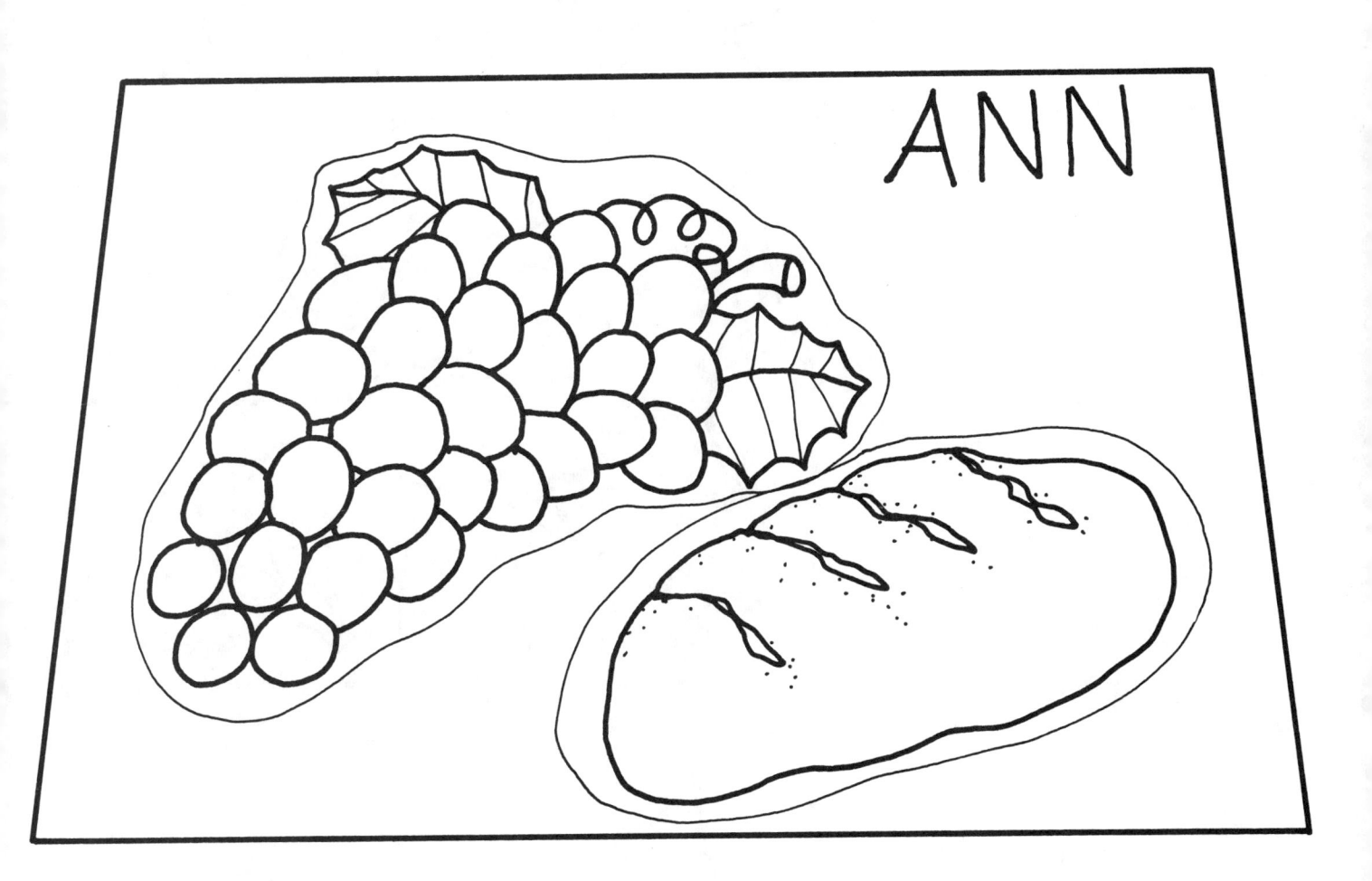

"The disciples left, went into the city and . . . prepared the Passover. When evening came, Jesus arrived with the Twelve."

Mark 14:16-17

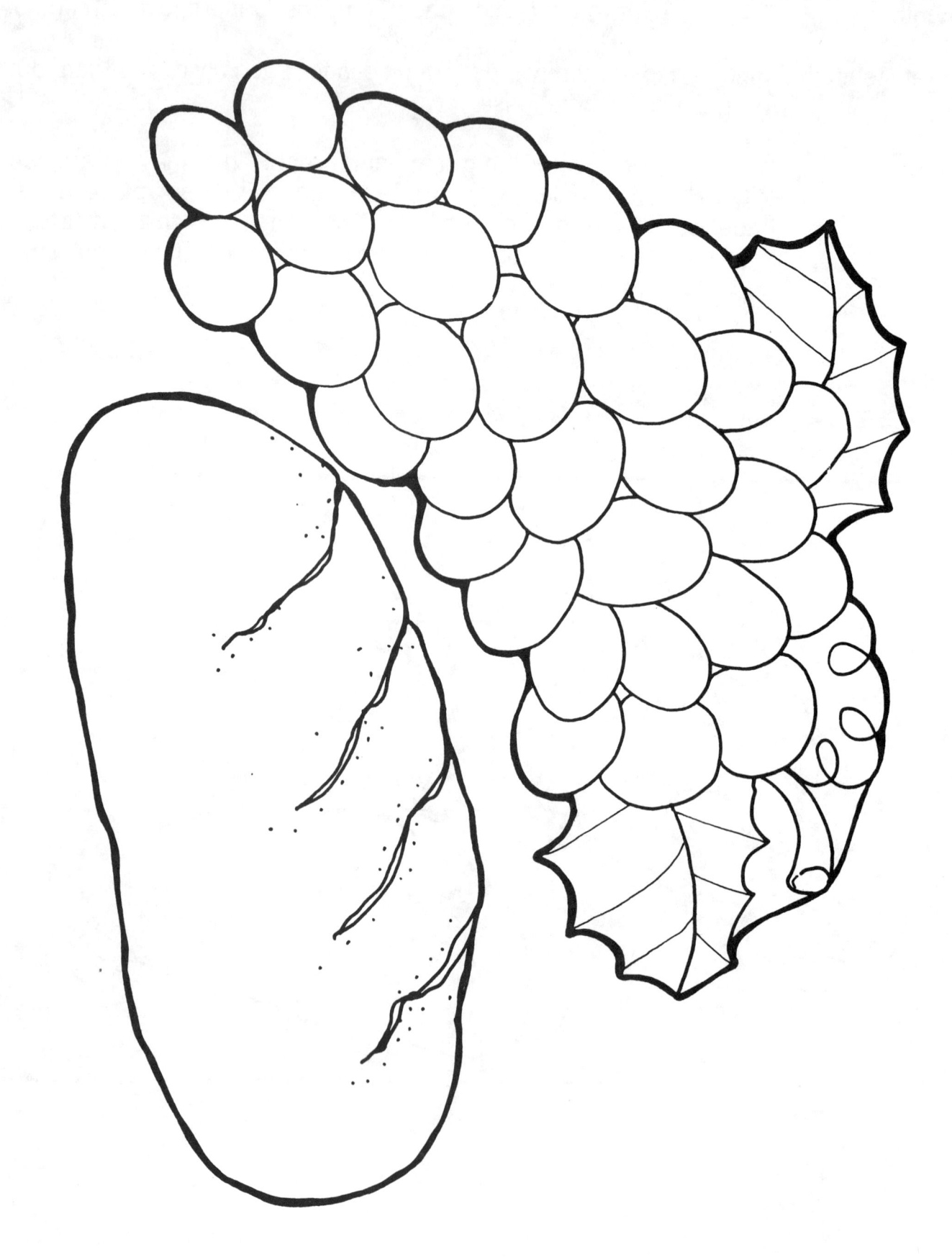

"'I tell you the truth,' Jesus answered, 'today–yes, tonight–before the rooster crows twice you yourself will disown me three times.'" Mark 14:30

OH, PETER!

Gather Up: 9" x 12" white construction paper, orange, yellow, brown, and red paper, crayons or markers, frilled paper meat crowns (optional), scissors, glue

Get Ready: Trace around each child's hand on white paper. Cut the colored paper into random, feathery shapes for the rooster's plumage.

Go: Let each child color a hand shape, and draw an eye on the thumb (which is the head). Help each glue on colored paper for feathers and a paper frill piece for a comb at the head. If desired, the rooster can be glued to construction paper and legs and feet drawn with markers.

CROWN OF THORNS

Gather Up: White paper plates, pattern, crayons, marker, paper, pen, scissors, glue, bulletin board

Get Ready: Cut the center from each paper plate. Make a copy of the two pattern pieces for each child. Cut small squares of paper.

Go: Have each child color two pattern pieces; then glue them to the sides of the plate to make a crown of thorns. Label each with the child's name. Mount the crowns of thorns on the bulletin board. Discuss what Jesus did to show His love for us. Ask children what they think they could do to be more kind or Christ-like. Write their ideas on small squares of paper and tack them to the board in the center of the crowns.

"The soldiers twisted together a crown of thorns . . . ." John 19:2a

"Jesus called out with a loud voice, 'Father, into your hands I commit my spirit.'"
Luke 23: 46a

JESUS ON THE CROSS

Gather Up: Craft sticks, small dried flowers or fabric flowers, glue, brushes

Get Ready: Set out the materials.

Go: Show children how to glue two craft sticks together in the shape of a cross. At the center of the cross they may glue some dried or fabric flowers. Let the crosses dry completely before handling.

Note: This craft will work best if you use thick, tacky glue and leave it to dry overnight.

"They found the stone rolled away from the tomb, but when they entered, they did not find the body of the Lord Jesus." Luke 24:2-3

JESUS IS RISEN!

Gather Up: Hard-boiled eggs, markers, food coloring, vinegar, bowls of hot water, glue, glitter

Get Ready: There is no way to resist the traditional craft of egg coloring when celebrating new life! Get the dyes ready, and let the kids try it!

Go: Print "Jesus Is Alive" on eggs, using markers, or decorate your eggs with dye. Squirt glue on some eggs in a random manner; then roll them in glitter. Don't forget to save some for egg salad sandwiches at snack time!

Gather Up: White paper, food coloring, glitter, straws, glue, black marker

Get Ready: Write "Jesus Is Risen!" across the top of the paper.

Go: Drop little puddles of food coloring on each paper. Let children blow through straws on the food coloring to make bursts of color. After these dry, children may wish to add glitter for bright, lively collages.

RESOURCES
PICTURE BOOKS

Brunelli, Robert, *The Macmillan Book of 366 Bible Stories*, New York: Macmillan Publishing Co., 1988.
Nice illustrations, short Bible stories for every day of the year, ranging in length from one paragraph to a few pages.

De Paola, Tomie, *The Parables of Jesus*, New York: Holiday House, 1987.
Cute interpretations of many parables such as The Lost Sheep, The Sower, and The Mustard Seed.

Helldorfer, M.C., *Daniel's Gift*, New York: Macmillan Publishing Co., 1990.
A young, sleepy shepherd has an adventure before he finally arrives at the stable to play his pipe for the newborn king.

Henderson, Florence and Shari Lewis, *One-Minute Bible Stories, New Testament*, New York: Doubleday, 1986.
Perfect for fidgety preschoolers. Each story is only a few paragraphs long with colorful illustrations.

Hewitt, Kathryn, *Two by Two, the Untold Story*, San Diego, CA: Harcourt Brace Jovanovich, 1984.
Excellent, whimsical story of how Noah, worried about getting the animals aboard, plans a terrific pleasure cruise.

Howard, Fern, *The Ten Commandments*, Auburn, ME: Ladybird Books, Inc., 1990.
The perfect little picture book for preschoolers, dealing with the weighty subject of the Ten Commandments but done in a very light tone and in a way that young children can understand.

Lewis, Shari, *One-Minute Bible Stories, New Testament*, New York: Doubleday, 1986.
Just the right length, with colorful illustrations.

Titherington, Jeannie, *A Child's Prayer*, New York: Greenwillow Books, 1989.
A soft and gentle prayer, with warm pictures, excellent for nap time.

RESOURCES
HANDS-ON CRAFTS AND ACTIVITIES

Currier, Mary, *Christian Crafts from Paper Plates*, Carthage, IL: Shining Star Publications, 1990.
Over three dozen Scripture-based craft projects to make from paper plates.

Stegena, Susan J., *Christian Crafts–Paper Bag Puppets*, Carthage, IL: Shining Star Publications, 1990.
This parade of paper bag puppets helps teach children Old and New Testament stories.

Daniel, Becky and contributors, *Biblical Performances for Early Childhood*, Carthage, IL: Shining Star Publications, 1990.
Biblical skits, pantomimes, and plays for ages 3-6.

Darling, Kathy, *Preschool Christian Value Lessons*, Carthage, IL: Shining Star Publications, 1991.
Activities, games, recipes, and creative crafts to nurture the development and awareness of the precious gifts of the Spirit.

Darling, Kathy, *Kids & Communities*, Palo Alto, CA: Monday Morning Books, 1989.
Easy crafts, familiar tunes, and patterns for props help children begin to see their importance and place in the family and in the wider community.

Lohf, Sabine, *Things I Can Make with Paper*, San Francisco, CA: Chronicle Books, 1987.
Quick paper crafts that you might be able to incorporate into your own lessons.

RESOURCES
FAMILIAR TUNES, MUSIC

Daniel, Becky and contributors, *Biblical Performances for Early Childhood*, Carthage, IL: Shining Star Publications, 1990.
Catchy lyrics set to familiar tunes.

Staines, Bill, *All God's Critters Got a Place in the Choir*, E.P. Dutton, 1989.
All God's critters make a joyful noise in this fun book.

Thigpen, Paul, *Come Sing God's Song*, Elgin, IL: David C. Cook Publishing Co., 1987.
Joyous book of praise and thankfulness; vibrant illustrations.